Mist of A Different Fire

"The Mingo George Story"

Carl Ellis

"He Ain't Heavy, He's My Brother"

The road is long
With many a winding turns
That leads us to who knows where
Who knows where

For I know
He would not encumber me
He ain't heavy, he's my brother

If I'm laden at all
I'm laden with sadness
That everyone's heart
Isn't filled with the gladness
Of love for one another

It's a long, long road
From which there is no return
While we're on the way to there
Why not share

He ain't heavy he's my brother

- Marcus Congleton, "The Hollies"

Dedicated
to the seeker of truth

Introduction

Here is the story of the Dilbone Massacre as it has never been told before: a complex story, profound in its' implications for the national characters of its subject, and rife with history lessons for today.

"Mist of A Different Fire: The Mingo George Story" includes an introduction, a chronology of events beginning 21,000 years ago and culminates that fateful day in Springcreek Township, Miami county of Ohio, August of 1813.

To understand the circumstances behind "Mingo George" and the Dillbone Massacre of Springcreek Township, Miami county, we will first go back in time and review events leading up to 1813 – "Snippets" in time - from the perspectives of both the pioneer settler and the aboriginal inhabitants of "Ohio Country"; and specifically, the lands that are present-day counties generally within western Ohio.

And while the scope of this work ends in 1813, the premise used throughout stems from the concept of

"Manifest Destiny" (the virtue of the American people and their institutions; the mission to spread these institutions, thereby redeeming and remaking the world in the image of the United States; the destiny under God to do this work).

The concept of "Manifest Destiny" obviously had serious consequences for the aboriginal peoples – in effect, assimilate or be annihilated.

Another possible influence under the concept of Manifest Destiny thought, is racial predominance, namely the idea that the American Anglo-Saxon race was "separate, innately superior" and "destined to bring good government, commercial prosperity and Christianity to the American continents and the world."

This view also held that "inferior races were doomed to subordinate status or extinction." This was used to justify "the expulsion and possible extermination of the Indians."

An early proponent of this idea was John Quincy Adams, a leading figure in U.S. expansion between the Louisiana

Purchase in 1803. Adams wrote to his father:

"The whole continent of North America appears to be destined by Divine Providence to be peopled by one nation, speaking one language, professing one general system of religious and political principles, and accustomed to one general tenor of social usages and customs."

To tie this history to the Dilbone Massacre, let us venture back in time then.... Beginning in a time when no "white man" was known to exist; a time when Indian culture was well-established and flourishing - long before European exploration of what would become the United States.

21000 - 18000 BCE

In 2008 researchers reported that DNA evidence indicated that 95% of native Americans had descended from 6 women of this period. It was believed that the women had lived in Beringia, a land bridge that stretched from Asia to North America during this time.

12300 BCE

In 2008 scientists reported that fossilized human feces found in 8 caves near Paisley, Ore., dated to about this time. The coprolites contained DNA with characteristics matching those of living Amerindians.

11000 BCE

In 2007 Alberto Nava, a California cave diver, and two Mexican dive buddies discovered a human skeleton in a deep underwater cave in Mexico's Yucatan jungle. In 2014 scientists said the skeleton was that of a young girl who probably fell into the cave about this time.

DNA evidence linked her to modern native Americans.

6000 BCE

The Wappo Indians settle in the area northern California around Mt. Konocti 8,000 years ago.

The Hokan Indians preceded the Miwoks in Northern California.

The Gabrielino-Tongva tribe lived in southern California about this time. Archaeologists in 2006 found their prehistoric milling area at the base of the Angeles National Forest estimated to be 8,000 years old.

200 – 1215 CE

The Fremont people lived in Utah and etched into rock designs of animals and people.

300 CE

The Anasazi inhabited the Canyon de Chelly and the Canyon del Muerto in northeast Arizona over this period.

600 CE

1300 Pueblo Indians built their Cliff Palace at Mesa Verde (Colorado).

750 CE

Native peoples in southwest Colorado started building stone houses above ground, first one-story, then two.

800 CE

Ohlone Indians occupied the cliffs near Mussel Rock, later Daly City, Ca., beginning from about this time.

1000 CE

The Cahokia settlement in Southern Illinois numbered about 30,000.

1000 CE

In Montana polychromatic rock drawings were made at Weatherman Draw, also known as the Valley of the Chiefs.

1400 Indians inhabited an area at the junction of 2 creeks between Walnut Creek and Lafayette, Ca. A burial site was found there in 1904. In 2004 some 80 sets of human remains was found during the construction of the Hidden Oaks housing development.

1050 CE

An Anasazi trade center in New Mexico offered pottery, turquoise and buffalo meat.

1150 CE

A group of Anasazi villages in southwest Colorado were suddenly abandoned during a period of severe drought. In 2000 evidence showed that a raiding party had swept through the area, killed the inhabitants and ate their flesh.

1170 CE

Madoc, a Welsh prince, is reputed to have discovered America. Many believe that he and his followers initially settled in the Georgia/Tennessee/ Kentucky area, eventually moving to the Upper Missouri, where they were assimilated into a tribe of the Mandans. New evidence is also emerging about a small band of Madoc's followers who remained in the Ohio area and are called "White Madoc."

1200 CE

The Anasazi in southwest Colorado began building their cliff dwellings at Mesa Verde about this time. The population thrived here for about 70 years making corrugated pottery and handsomely decorated black and white pottery.

1250 CE

The Anasazi in southwest Colorado fought a battle against unknown enemies.

The number of kivas (*a large chamber, often wholly or partly underground, in a Pueblo Indian village, used for religious ceremonies and other purposes*) built was greatly increased.

Quality of workmanship in building decreased.

People began to leave.

1275 CE

Indian settlers built a town called Atsina on top of El Morro (New Mexico).

1300 CE

The Anasazi Indian culture of the American southwest, some 15 to 20 thousand people, disappeared from the Four Corners region (*The Four Corners is a region of the United States consisting of the southwestern corner of Colorado northwestern corner of New Mexico northeastern corner of Arizona and southeastern corner of Utah The Four Corners area is named after the quadripoint where the boundaries of the four states meet*) by this time.

All the Anasazi were gone from Mesa Verde. They probably moved south and broke up into present-day Pueblo tribes. *(Anasazi means enemy ancestors in Navajo.)*

1300 CE

The Mississippian people, the largest pre-Columbian culture north of Mexico, built the earthen city of Cahokia about this time.

The Arapaho and Cheyenne Indian Nations settled the Colorado area.

1350 CE

The Fremont Indians, who had lived in Utah's Range Creek Canyon since about 200, disappeared from the archeological record.

1494 CE

Columbus began the practice using Indians as slaves.

1513 CE

Spanish explorer Juan Ponce de León lands on the coast of Florida.

1536 CE

Jacques Cartier sailed for France from Canada and carried with him the kidnapped local chief Donnacona, who later died in France. Donnacona, prior to his death, described a mythical kingdom with great riches called Saguenay.

1540 CE

Hernando de Soto reached southern Georgia. He found the Indians there raising tame turkeys, caged opossums, corn, beans, pumpkins, cucumbers and plums.

1540 CE

Hernando de Soto fought native Indians at the bloody battle of Mabila in present day Alabama.

1541 CE

Spanish explorer Hernando de Soto discovered and crossed the Mississippi River, which he called Rio de Espiritu Santo.

He encountered the Cherokee Indians, who numbered about 25,000 and inhabited the area from the Ohio River to the north to the Chattahoochee in present day Georgia, and from the valley of the Tennessee east across the Great Smoky Mountains to the Piedmont of the Carolinas.

1542 CE

New laws were passed in Spain giving protection against the enslavement of Indians in America.

1559 CE

1,500 Spanish settlers sailed from Vera Cruz to found a settlement on Pensacola Bay in Florida, but were repulsed by hostile Indians.

1565 CE

Saint Augustine, Florida, settled by the Spanish, becomes the first permanent European colony in North America.

1565 CE

Spanish fleet forces under Pedro Menendez de Aviles massacred a band of 350 French Huguenots at Fort Caroline in Florida who posed a potential threat to Spanish dominance in the area.

They also took advantage of the local Timucuan Indian tribe.

Artist Jacques Le Moyne de Morgues managed to escape and return to France, where he painted watercolors depicting the local botany.

His alleged paintings of Indians living nearby were later thrown into question.

1566 CE

Spanish conquistador Juan Pardo arrived the Spanish settlement at Santa Elena, on what later became known as Parris Island, South Carolina.

He marched into the interior and founded Fort San Juan next to a Catawba town called Joara.

Fort San Juan was burned down by the Catawba after about 18 months.

1571 CE

All eight members of a Jesuit mission in Virginia were murdered by Indians who pretended to be their friends.

1604 CE

French explorer Samuel de Champlain, Pierre Dugua and 77 others landed on the island of St. Croix and made friends with the native Passamaquoddy Indians. It later became part of Maine on the US-Canadian border.

1604 CE

Captain Christopher Newport and 105 followers founded - established by the London Company - Jamestown on the mouth of the James River in Virginia.

They had left England with 144 members, 39 died on the way over.

The colony was near the large Indian village of Werowocomoco, home of Pocahontas, the daughter Powhatan, an Algonquin chief.

In 2003 archeologists believed that they had found the site of Werowocomoco, where Powhatan resided from 1607-1609.

1607 CE

Some 200 Indian warriors stormed the unfinished stockade at Jamestown, Va. Two settlers were killed and 10 seriously wounded before they were repulsed by cannon fire from the colonists' 3 moored ships.

1607 CE

Colonists in North America completed James Fort in Jamestown.

Hostilities with the Indians ended as ambassadors said their emperor, Powhatan, had commanded local chiefs to live in peace with the English.

1608 CE

John Smith met with the Indian emperor Powhatan at Werocomoco on the Pamunkey River.

He studied the Powhattan language and culture.

The Powhatan were an aggressive tribe and under Chief Powhatan's leadership, they had conquered and subjugated more than 20 other tribes.

Pocahontas was a Powhattan Indian girl of 10-11 years when she knew Smith in Virginia.

1613 CE

The colonists at Jamestown kidnapped Pocahontas and held her for ransom to force her father to free some English hostages and to return some stolen tools.

1614 CE

American Indian princess Pocahontas married English Jamestown colonist John Rolfe in Virginia.

Their marriage brought a temporary peace between the English settlers and the Algonquians.

1616 CE

The French explorer Samuel de Champlain arrived to winter in a Huron Indian village after being wounded in a battle with Iroquois in New France.

1616 CE

A smallpox epidemic decimates the New England Native American population.

1616 CE

American Indian princess Pocahontas and her husband, Jamestown colonist John Rolfe, sailed to England with their infant son.

1617 CE

Pocahontas, American Indian princess, attended a court masque *(a form of aristocratic entertainment usually performed in English courts in the 16th and 17th centuries, originally consisting of pantomime and dancing)* with King James I and Queen Anne.

1617 CE

As Pocahontas and John Rolfe prepared to sail back to Virginia, she died reportedly of either small pox or pneumonia.

Pocahontas (Rebecca Rolfe) was buried at the parish church of St. George in Gravesend, England.

1619 CE

The House of Burgess, the first representative assembly in America, meets for the first time in Virginia.

The first African slaves are brought to Jamestown.

1619 CE

An epidemic, possibly viral hepatitis from contact with Europeans, ravaged the Wampanoag confederacy in Massachusetts. This helped to make possible the Pilgrim settlement in 1620.

1620 CE

The Plymouth Colony in Massachusetts is established by Pilgrims from England.

Before disembarking from their ship, the Mayflower, 41 male passengers sign the Mayflower Compact, an agreement that forms the basis of the colony's government.

1621 CE

The first American Thanksgiving was held in Massachusetts' Plymouth colony in 1621 to give thanks for a bountiful harvest.

51 Pilgrims were introduced to cranberries by Wampanoag and served codfish, sea bass and turkeys while their 90 Wampanoag guests contributed venison during the three-day feast.

After the survival of their first colony through a bitter winter and the subsequent gathering of the harvest in the autumn, Plymouth Colony Governor William Bradford issued a thanksgiving proclamation.

1622 CE

The Powhattan Confederacy attacked and massacred 350 colonists in and around the outlying settlements of Jamestown, Virginia - one-fourth of the population.

1626 CE

Peter Minuit arrives in New Netherland and later buys Manhattan from the Native Americans for items worth approximately $24. He then names the island New Amsterdam.

[Publisher's sidebar: According to modern-day writers, "One of the most persistent myths in American history is that European explorers really got one over on the Native Americans by purchasing the entire island of Manhattan for a measly $24 worth of beads and trinkets.

It seems like the ultimate bargain, but the truth of the story is more complicated and murkier than that.

In the Dutch National Archives is the only known primary reference to the Manhattan sale: a letter written by Dutch merchant Pieter Schage on November 5, 1626, to directors of the West India Company, which was instrumental in the exploration and settlement of "New Netherland."

In the letter, he writes, "They have purchased the Island of Manhattes from the savages for the value of 60 guilders.

Nineteenth century historians converted those 60 guilders to U.S. dollars and got what was then $24.

That same figure has been repeated for almost two centuries since, frozen in time and untouched by changes to the value of currency—but those guilders don't stand at $24 today.

According to information from the International Institute of Social History at the Royal Netherlands Academy of Arts and Sciences, 60 guilders in 1626 was equivalent to....$951.08 USD.

While $951.08 is less of a steal than $24, there are still some other confounding factors to the deal.

For one thing, Schagen's letter does not mention who actually made the deal with the Dutch or the tribe on whose behalf it was sold, and the deed for the land has been lost.

Without confirmation from a primary source, historians are left to infer who the island was purchased from, and can't seem to agree.

A few accounts say that the Dutch got the wool pulled over their eyes, and bought the land from a group of natives that lived on Long Island and were only traveling through Manhattan. Coming upon the European rubes, they traded away land they had no claim to and continued on home with the Dutch loot.

Another detail that Schagen leaves out of his letter is what the Dutch actually used to make the purchase. He says only that they traded "for the value of 60 guilders," but doesn't specify if that was actual Dutch coins, native currency, food, or other goods.

It certainly doesn't mention any beads.

The purchase of Staten Island a few decades later has more surviving documentation, including the deed, which says the Dutch traded "10 boxes of shirts, 10 ells of red cloth, 30 pounds of powder, 30 pairs of socks, 2 pieces of duffel, some awls, 10 muskets, 30 kettles, 25 adzes, 10 bars of lead, 50 axes and some knives."

If the Manhattan trade was made with similar goods, the Native Americans got less shafted than legend implies, and received 60 guilders worth of useful equipment and what was high-end technology at the time.

Also missing with the deed or any additional documentation of the sale are records of any intangibles that might have been traded with the 60 guilders worth of whatever it was. Early Dutch settlements in the area were established to participate in fur trade with the natives, and whichever tribe made the Manhattan deal likely could have counted on the Dutch as trade partners and potential allies in the future, making the deal that much sweeter.

One last thing to consider—which further complicates the

story of the Manhattan deal—is the ideological difference between the Europeans and the Native Americans regarding the sale of land.

The sale may seem particularly lopsided, even aside from the small price tag, because of the popular conception that the Native Americans didn't think of the land as property or something that could be traded, and had no idea what they were getting into.

But that's not accurate.

"European settlers and early Americans misunderstood tribal economies and property rights," says Robert J. Miller, a specialist in American Indian law at the Lewis & Clark Law School, in the Oregon Law Review.

"Even today, there seems to be an almost universal misunderstanding that the American Indian culture had and still have no appreciation or understanding of private property ownership and private, free market, capitalist economic activities. This mistaken idea could not be further from the truth."

In reality, Miller says, American Indians were continuously involved in free market trade situations before and after European contact and, while most of the land that Indians lived on was considered tribal land owned by the tribe or by all the tribe's members in common, almost all the tribes recognized various forms of permanent or semi-permanent private rights to land.

Individual tribe members could, and did, acquire and exercise use rights over specific pieces of land (tribal and not), homes, and valuable plants like berry patches and fruit and nut trees, both through inheritable rights and by buying and selling.

In 'Law in American History: Volume 1', law professor G. Edward White interprets the Manhattan "sale" from the Indians' point of view as "not relinquishing the island, but simply welcoming the Dutch as additional occupants," in the context of a property rights system that was different from the Europeans', but not nonexistent.

He thinks they "allowed the Dutch to exercise what they thought of as hunting or use rights on the island" and assumed continuing rights of their own, in which case the deal seems much better for the Indians than legend would have us believe"].

1628 CE

A May festival in Quincy, Mass., degenerated into an orgy with Indian women.

1630 CE

Indians introduced pilgrims to popcorn at Thanksgiving.

1630 CE

New Amsterdam's governor bought Gull Island from Indians for cargo and renamed it Oyster Island. It later became Ellis Island.

1632 CE

The French explorer Etienne Brule was killed by the Huron Indians for unknown reasons.

1636 CE

Roger Williams and his followers founded Providence, Rhode Island, on land purchased from the Narragansett Indians. The settlement was governed by policies of democracy and religious tolerance.

1636 CE

John Oldham, trader in Mass., was murdered by Indians. Open warfare begins with Pequot Indians.

1637 CE

The Connecticut, Massachusetts Bay, and Plymouth colonists militia and their Mohegan allies killed over 600 Pequot Indians at their village at Mystic.

After numerous encounters, the tribe is virtually eliminated.

The survivors were parceled out to other tribes. Those given to the Mohegans eventually became the Mashantucket Pequots.

1642 CE

Dutch settlers slaughtered lower Hudson Valley Indians in New Netherland, North America, who sought refuge from Mohawk attackers. The Hudson Valley Indians had been making raids against the colony.

Both sides will later sign a truce that will last a year.

1643 CE

Roger Williams of Providence, Rhode Island, published "A Key into the Language of America," a dictionary of the Narragansett Indian language and a commentary on the culture and customs of the southern New England Indians.

1645 CE

- The Dutch and the Hudson River Valley Indians conclude peace after four years of warfare.

- The New England Confederation sign a peace treaty with the Naragansett Indians.

- Settlers in New Amsterdam gained peace with the Indians after conducting talks with the Mohawks.

1646 CE

The 1st Protestant church assembly for Indians took place in Massachusetts.

1649 CE

Iroquois attacks and starvation decimated the Huron nation from some 12,000 to a few hundred.

1653 CE

The Iroquois League signed a peace treaty with the French, vowing not to wage war with other tribes under French protection.

1656 CE

A party of Oneida Indians killed 3 Frenchmen near Montreal.

In response Gov. Gen. Louis d'Ailleboust arrested a hunting party of 12 Mohawks and Onondagas and ordered the arrest of all Iroquois in the French colonies.

1659 CE

Cornelius Meylin, patroon of Staten Island, wrote in his recollections that Staten Island was acquired in 1630 in exchange for "kittles, axes, Hoos, wampum, drilling awles, Jews Harps and diverse small wares."

1675 CE

Three Wampanoag Indians were hanged in Plymouth, Massachusetts. On the testimony of a Native American witness, Plymouth Colony arrested three Wampanoags, including a counselor to Metacom, a Pokanoket sachem. A jury among whom were some Indian members convicted them of the recent murder of John Sassamon, an advisor to Metacom.

1675 CE

King Philip's War erupts in New England between colonists and Native Americans as a result of tensions over colonist's expansionist activities, as well as retaliation (Native Americans massacred colonists at Swansea, Plymouth colony) of the Native Americans for the execution of three of their people who had been charged with murder by the English.

The bloody war rages up and down the Connecticut River valley (Abenaki, Massachusetts, Mohegan & Wampanoag Indians formed an anti-English front) in

Massachusetts and in the Plymouth and Rhode Island colonies, expending to include the Norwottock, Pocumtuck and Agawam warriors, eventually resulting in 600 English colonials and 3,000 Native Americans being killed - including women and children - on both sides.

In New Hampshire and Maine, the Saco Indians continue to raid settlements for another year and a half.

1676 CE

- In King Philip's War, Narragansett and Nipmuck Indians raided Lancaster, Mass. Over 35 villagers were killed and 24 were taken captive.
- Wampanoag allies including Narragansetts destroyed Providence, Rhode Island.
- The house of Roger Williams was destroyed as he negotiated with Indian leaders on the outskirts of town.
- Sudbury, Massachusetts, was attacked by Indians.

- King Philip (the colonist's nickname for Metacomet, chief of the Wampanoags) is hunted down and killed by English soldiers on August 12, 1676, in a swamp in Rhode Island, ending the war in southern New England and ending the independent power of Native Americans there.
- In June, the colonists with the Mohegan Indians defeat King Philip's men at Hadley.
- King Philip's War ends on August 22 when the Indians surrender.

1680 CE

War started when the Spanish were expelled from Santa Fe, New Mexico, by Indians under Chief Pope.

1680 CE

Pueblo Indians took possession of Santa Fe, N.M., after driving out the Spanish. They destroyed almost all of the Spanish churches in Taos and Santa Fe.

1680 CE

Kateri Tekakwitha (b.1656), known as the "Lily of the Mohawks," died in Canada.

She was born to a pagan Iroquois father and an Algonquin Christian mother in upstate New York.

Her parents and only brother died when she was 4 during a smallpox epidemic that left her badly scarred and with impaired eyesight.

She went to live with her uncle, a Mohawk, and was baptized Catholic by Jesuit missionaries.

But she was ostracized and persecuted by other natives for her faith.

In 2012 she was named a saint in the Catholic church.

1683 CE

William Penn signed a friendship treaty with Lenni Lenape (Delaware) Indians in Pennsylvania. It became the only treaty "not sworn to, nor broken."

1686 CE

The Lenape Indians allegedly sold land along the Lehigh River to William Penn.

1690 CE

The beginning of King William's War as hostilities in Europe between the French and English spill over to the colonies.

Some 200 French and Indian troops burned Schenectady, NY, and massacred about 60 people to avenge Iroquois raids on Canada.

These combined forces of the French and the Indians attack towns in New York, Maine, New Hampshire, and Massachusetts.

"Sell a country? Why not sell the air, the great sea, as well as the Earth? Did not the Great Spirit make them all for the use of his children?" --Tecumseh, SHAWNEE

"The White Man's way is to possess, control, and divide. It has always been difficult for Indian people to understand this.

There are certain things we cannot own that must be shared. The Land is one of these things.

We need to relook at what we are doing to the Earth. We are digging in her veins and foolishly diminishing the natural resources. We are not living in balance.

We do not own the Earth; the Earth owns us. Today, let us ponder the true relationship between the Earth and ourselves.

Great Spirit, today, let me see the Earth as You would have me see Her."

- Elder's Meditation of the Day May 31, 2014

1700 CE

Several dozen members of the Calusa Indian tribe, nicknamed "The Fierce Ones," escaped from Florida to Cuba in the early 1700s after Spanish soldiers and other tribes overran their region.

1702 CE

In March, Queen Anne ascends the English throne.

In May, England declares war on France after the death of the King of Spain, Charles II, to stop the union of France and Spain.

This War of the Spanish Succession is called Queen Anne's War in the colonies, where the English and American colonists will battle the French, their Native American allies, and the Spanish for the next eleven years.

1704 CE

English forces attacked Apalachee Indians in Florida driving them into slavery and exile. Some 800 Apalachee fled west to French-held Mobile.

1711 CE

Following white encroachment, and enslaving of Indian children hostilities escalate to war between Native Americans and settlers in North Carolina after the massacre of settlers there.

1715 CE Apr 15

Uprising of Yamasse Indians in South Carolina.

1722 CE

The original Iroquois League, often known as the Five Nations (the Mohawk, Oneida, Onondaga, Cayuga, and Seneca nations) became the Six Nations after the Tuscarora nation joined the League.

1725 CE Feb 20

New Hampshire militiamen partook in the first recorded scalping of Indians by whites in North America. 10 sleeping Indians were scalped by whites for scalp bounty.

1729 CE Nov 28

Natchez Indians massacred most of the 300 French settlers and soldiers at Fort Rosalie, Louisiana.

1730 CE

The French arrived in Swanton, Vermont, and the plague followed. The local Abenaki Indians faded into the woods.

1736 CE May 26

In northwestern Mississippi, British and Chickasaw Indians defeated a combined force of French soldiers and Choctaw Indians at the Battle of Ackia, thus opening the region to English settlement.

1736 CE Aug 8

Mahomet Weyonomon, a Mohegan sachem or leader, died of smallpox while waiting to see King George II to complain directly about British settlers encroaching on tribal lands in the Connecticut colony.

The tribal chief was buried in an unmarked grave in a south London churchyard.

1749 CE

Pierre-Joseph Celron, sieur de Bienville, with 200 to 250 French soldiers and some Indians, was sent in 1749 to renew and strengthen France's claim to the Ohio country and drive out the British.

During navigation of the Allegheny, Ohio and Great Miami rivers, he buried lead plates near the city of present-day Hamilton, Ohio, with the text declaring the French land claim.

He also sought Indian cooperation in the fur trade.

1750 CE

Teedyuscung, a Lenape Indian, joined the Christian mission of Gnadenhutten, founded by Swiss Moravian settlers in the Lehigh Valley town of Bethlehem.

1750 CE

The Ais Indians of Florida were wiped out. In 2004 a site on Hutchinson Island, inhabited by the Ais, revealed 2 thousand year old burials.

1754 CE

Teedyuscung, a Lenape (*aka: Cherokee*) Indian, joined the Iroquois Indians in the Wyoming Valley along the banks of the Susquehanna River.

1754 CE

The French and Indian War erupts as a result of disputes over land in the Ohio River Valley.

In May, George Washington leads a small group of American colonists to victory over the French, then builds Fort Necessity in the Ohio territory.

In July, after being attacked by numerically superior French forces, Washington surrenders the fort and retreats.

1754 CE

Col. George Washington led a 40-man detachment that defeated French and Indian forces in a skirmish near Great Meadows, Pa.

1754 CE

The Albany Congress opened. New York colonial Gov. George Clinton called for the meeting to discuss better relations with Indian tribes and common defensive measures against the French.

The attendees included Indians and representatives from Connecticut, Maryland, Massachusetts, New Hampshire, New York, Pennsylvania and Rhode Island.

Benjamin Franklin attended and presented his Plan of Union, which was adopted by the conference.

The meeting ended after 30-days deliberations.

1754 CE

George Washington surrendered the small, circular Fort Necessity (later Pittsburgh) in southwestern Pennsylvania to the French, leaving them in control of the Ohio Valley.

This marked the beginning of the French and Indian War also called the 7 Years' War.

1754 CE

The Gnadenhutten mission, Pa., was attacked by renegade Lenape Indians and 11 white people were killed.

1755 CE

In February, English General Edward Braddock arrives in Virginia with two regiments of English troops.

Gen. Braddock assumes the post of commander in chief of all English forces in America.

In April, Gen. Braddock and Lt. Col. George Washington set out with nearly 2000 men to battle the French in the Ohio territory.

In July, a force of about 900 French and Indians defeat those English forces.

Braddock is mortally wounded.

Massachusetts Governor William Shirley then becomes the new commander in chief.

1755 CE

General Edward Braddock was mortally wounded when French and Indian troops ambushed his force of British regulars and colonial militia, which was on its way to attack France's Fort Duquesne (Pittsburgh).

Gen. Braddock's troops were decimated at Fort Duquesne, where he refused to accept George Washington's advice on frontier style fighting. British Gen'l. Braddock gave his bloody sash to George Washington at Fort Necessity just before he died on Jul 13.

1755 CE

British forces under William Johnson and 250 Indians defeated the French and their allied Indians at the Battle of Lake George, NY.

1755 CE Dec 31

Teedyuscung, a Lenape Indian, led 30 Lenape Indians on a raid against English plantations along the Delaware River.

Over the next few days his band killed 7 men and took 5 prisoners.

1756 CE

England declares war on France, as the French and Indian War in the colonies now spreads to Europe.

1756 CE Apr 14

Gov. Glen of South Carolina protested against 900 Acadia Indians.

1756 CE May 17

After a year and a half of undeclared war Britain declared war on France, beginning the French and Indian War.

England hoped to conquer Canada.

The final defeat of the French came in 1763 with the British victory at the Battle of Quebec on the Plains of Abraham.

1756 CE Nov 12

Teedyuscung, a Lenape Indian, spoke with Gov. Denny at Easton, Pa., to discuss grievances.

1757 CE

In June, William Pitt becomes England's Secretary of State and escalates the French and Indian War in the colonies by establishing a policy of unlimited warfare.

In July, Benjamin Franklin begins a five year stay in London.

1758 CE Jul 8

During the French and Indian War a British attack on Fort Carillon at Ticonderoga, New York, was foiled by the French.

Some 3,500 Frenchmen defeated the British army of 15,000, which lost 2,000 men.

1758 CE Aug 29

New Jersey Legislature formed the 1st Indian reservation consisting of 3,000 acres..

1758 CE Nov 25

In the French and Indian War British forces under General John Forbes captured Fort Duquesne (the site of present day Pittsburgh, est. 1754).

George Washington participated in the campaign.

Forbes renamed the site Fort Pitt after William Pitt the Elder, who directed British military policy in the Seven Years' War of 1756-'63.

Before his arrival, the French had burned the fort and retreated.

1758 CE

In July, a devastating defeat occurs for English forces at Lake George, New York, as nearly two thousand men are lost during a frontal attack against well entrenched French forces at Fort Ticonderoga.

French losses are 377. In November, the French abandon Fort Duquesne in the Ohio territory.

Settlers then rush into the territory to establish homes.

Also in 1758, the first Indian reservation in America is founded, in New Jersey, on 3000 acres.

1759 CE Jul 26

The French relinquished Fort Carillon in New York, to the British under General Jeffrey Amherst.

The British changed the name to Fort Ticonderoga, from the Iroquois word Cheonderoga (land between the waters).

1759 CE

French Fort Niagara is captured by the English. Also in 1759, war erupts between Cherokee Indians and southern colonists.

1760 CE Feb 16

Cherokee Indians held hostage at Fort St. George, SC, were killed in revenge for Indian attacks on frontier settlements.

1760 CE Aug 7

Ft. Loudon, Tennessee, surrendered to Cherokee Indians.

1761 CE

French and Indians forces in the Ohio Valley were defeated.

1761 CE

In western North Carolina British soldiers razed Kituwha, the heart of the Cherokee Nation. Punitive raids here were repeated in 1776.

1761 CE

The Proclamation of 1763, signed by King George III of England, prohibits any English settlement west of the Appalachian mountains and requires those already settled in those regions to return east in an attempt to ease tensions with Native Americans.

1763 CE

The French and Indian War, known in Europe as the Seven Year's War, ends with the Treaty of Paris.

Under the treaty, France gives England all French territory east of the Mississippi River, except New Orleans.

The Spanish give up east and west Florida to the English in return for Cuba.

1763 CE

In May, the Ottawa Native Americans under Chief Pontiac begin all-out warfare against the British west of Niagara, destroying several British forts and conducting a siege against the British at Detroit.

In August, Pontiac's forces are defeated by the British near Pittsburgh.

The siege of Detroit ends in November, but hostilities between the British and Chief Pontiac continue for several years.

1763 CE Feb 10

Britain, Spain and France signed the Treaty of Paris ending the Seven Years' War, aka the French-Indian War.

France ceded Canada to England and gave up all her territories in the New World except New Orleans and a few scattered islands including St. Pierre and Miquelon off the coast of Newfoundland.

1763 CE Apr 19

Teedyuscung, a Lenape Indian leader, burned to death while sleeping in his cabin in the Wyoming Valley, Pa.

The fire destroyed the whole Indian village.

A few days later settlers from Connecticut arrived to resume their construction of a town.

1763 CE May 7

Indian chief Pontiac began his attack on a British fort in present-day Detroit, Michigan.

1763 CE Jul 24

Ottawa Chief Pontiac led an uprising in the wild, distant lands that would one day become Michigan, Ohio and Pennsylvania.

1763 CE Oct 7

George III of Great Britain issued a royal proclamation reserving for the crown the right to acquire land from western tribes.

This closed lands in North America north and west of Alleghenies to white settlement and ended the acquisition efforts of colonial land syndicates.

The Royal Proclamation of 1763 guaranteed Indian rights to land and self-government.

1763 CE

British forces, under orders from Sir Jeffrey Amherst, distributed smallpox-infected blankets among American Indians in the 1st known case of its use as a biological weapon.

1764 CE Nov 16

Indians surrendered to British in Indian War of Chief Pontiac.

1764 CE

The Sugar Act is passed by the English Parliament to offset the war debt brought on by the French and Indian War and to help pay for the expenses of running the colonies and newly acquired territories.

This act increases the duties on imported sugar and other items such as textiles, coffee, wines and indigo (dye).

It doubles the duties on foreign goods reshipped from England to the colonies and also forbids the import of foreign rum and French wines.

1766 CE Jul 24

At Fort Ontario, Canada, Ottawa chief Pontiac and William Johnson signed a peace agreement.

1766 CE

Jonathan Carver, an American-born British army officer, set out to cross the American continent, but was stopped in Minnesota by a war between the Sioux and Chippewa.

1767 CE Oct 9

The survey party of Mason and Dixon came to a halt after 233 miles when Indians of the Six Nations said they had "reached the end of their commission".

1767 CE

British explorer Jonathan Carver described petrographic images of snakes and buffalo near a cave at bluffs in Minnesota called Wakan Tipi by the Dakota people. The area later became part of St. Paul.

1768 CE

Tecumseh, statesman, warrior and Patriot was born March 1768, three miles west of Springfield, Ohio, Clark County, close to present-day Route 40 and State Route 369 - at the Shawnee Indian Town called Piqua. Site of the battle of Piqua, August 8th, 1780, presently George Rogers Clark Memorial Park.

As a leader of the Shawnee tribe and a spokesman for the Western Indian he resolutely resisted encroachment on their territory.

Through his efforts and under his leadership the Indian Tribes for a time combined in confederation in an attempt to create an Indian Nation in the Ohio Valley - Great Lakes Area. He disappeared while leading the combined Indian force at the battle of the Thames, October 5th, 1813.

1768 CE Nov 5

William Johnson, the northern Indian Commissioner, signed a treaty with the Iroquois Indians to acquire much of the land between the Tennessee and Ohio rivers for future settlement.

1769 CE Apr 20

Ottawa Chief Pontiac (b~1720) was murdered by an Indian in Cahokia.

1773 CE

May 10, the Tea Act takes effect. It maintains a threepenny per pound import tax on tea arriving in the colonies, which had already been in effect for six years.

It also gives the near bankrupt British East India Company a virtual tea monopoly by allowing it to sell directly to colonial agents, bypassing any middlemen, thus underselling American merchants.

The East India Company had successfully lobbied Parliament for such a measure.

In September, Parliament authorizes the company to ship half a million pounds of tea to a group of chosen tea agents.

1763 CE

About 8000 Bostonians (colonial patriots) gather to hear Sam Adams tell them Royal Governor Hutchinson has repeated his command not to allow the ships out of the harbor until the tea taxes are paid.

That night, the Boston Tea Party occurs as colonial activists disguise themselves as Mohawk Indians then board the ships and dump all 342 containers of tea into the harbor.

1775 CE

Richard Henderson, a North Carolina judge, representing the Transylvania Company, met with three Cherokee Chiefs (Oconistoto, chief warrior and first representative of the Cherokee Nation or tribe of Indians, Attacuttuillah and Sewanooko) to purchase (for the equivalent of $50,000) all the land lying between the Ohio, Kentucky and Cumberland rivers; some 17 to 20 million acres.

It was known as the Treaty of Sycamore Shoals or The Henderson Purchase. The purchase was later declared invalid but land cession was not reversed.

1776 CE

Spanish explorers encountered the native Havasupai Indians in Arizona.

1777 CE Nov 15

The Continental Congress approved the Articles of Confederation, precursor to the U.S. Constitution.

The structure of the Constitution was inspired by the Iroquois Confederacy of six major northeastern tribes.

The matriarchal society of the Iroquois later inspired the suffragist movement.

1778 CE Aug 31

British killed 17 Stockbridge Indians in Bronx during Revolution.

1778 CE Sept 7

Shawnee Indians attacked and laid siege to Boonesborough, Kentucky.

1778 CE Sept 17

The 1st treaty between the US and Indian tribes, Treaty with the Delawares, was signed at Fort Pitt.

Synopsis of Treaty:
- *All offenses mutually forgiven.*
- *Peace and friendship perpetual.*
- *In case of war, each party to assist the other.*
- *United States to have free passage to forts or towns of their enemies.*

- Such warriors as can be spared, to join the troops of the United States.

- Neither party to inflict punishment without an impartial trial.

- Nor protect criminal fugitives, etc.

- Agent to be appointed by the United States to trade with the Delaware Nation.

- United States guarantee to them all territorial rights as bounded by former treaties.

- To have a representation in Congress on certain conditions.

1778 CE Nov 11

Indians, led by William Butler, massacred the inhabitants of Cherry Valley, N.Y.

1782 CE

Smallpox, reduced the Mandans, a Missouri River tribe of 40,000 people, down to 2,000 survivors.

1782 CE Mar 8

The Gnadenhutten massacre took place as some 90 Christian Delaware Indians were slain by militiamen in Ohio in retaliation for raids carried out by other Indians.

1784 CE

The British gave their Indian allies from New York a large parcel of land southwest of Toronto after they fled to Canada following the American war of independence.

(In 2006 the Six Nations Iroquois Confederacy claimed that part of this land had been sold without their proper consent for a new housing development in Caledonia.)

1784 CE

Treaty with the Six Nations *(Synopsis)*
Six American Indian hostages to be immediately delivered and are in custody of US until all prisoners freed.

The Oneida and Tuscarora nations shall be secured in the possession of the lands on which they are settled. A line shall be drawn, beginning at the mouth of a creek about four miles east of Niagara, called Oyonwavea, or Johnston's Landing-Place, upon the lake named by the Indians Oswego, and by us Ontario.

From thence southerly in a direction always four miles east of the carrying-path, between Lake Erie and Ontario, to the mouth of Tehoseroron or Buffaloe Creek on Lake Erie.

Thence south to the north boundary of the state of Pennsylvania. Thence west to the end of the said north boundary.

Thence south along the west boundary of the said state, to the river Ohio; the said line from the mouth of the Oyonwayea to the Ohio, shall be the western boundary of the lands of the Six Nations, so that the Six Nations shall and do yield to the United States, all claims to the country west of the said boundary, and then they shall be secured in the peaceful possession of the lands they inhabit east and north of the same, reserving only six miles square round the fort of Oswego, to the United States, for the support of the same.

The Commissioners of the United States, in consideration of the present circumstances of the Six Nations, and in execution of the humane and liberal views of the United States upon the signing of the above articles, will order goods to be delivered to the said Six Nations for their use and comfort.

1785 CE Jan 21

Chippewa, Delaware, Ottawa and Wyandot Indians signed a treaty of Fort McIntosh, ceding present-day Ohio to the United States.

Full text:
Treaty with the Wyandot, etc.,

Articles of a treaty concluded at Fort M'Intosh, the twenty-first day of January, one thousand seven hundred and eighty-five, between the Commissioners Plenipotentiary of the United States of America, of the one Part, and the Sachems and Warriors of the Wiandot, Delaware, Chippawa arid Ottawa Nations of the other.

The Commissioners Plenipotentiary of the United States in Congress assembled, give peace to the Wiandot, Delaware, Chippewa. and Ottawa nations of Indians, on the following conditions:

ARTICLE I.

Three chiefs, one from among the Wiandot, and two from among the Delaware nations, shall be delivered up to the Commissioners of the United States, to be by them retained till all the prisoners, white and black, taken by the said nations, or any of them, shall be restored.

ARTICLE II.

The said Indian nations do acknowledge themselves and all their tribes to be under the protection of the United States and of no other sovereign whatsoever.

ARTICLE III.

The boundary line between the United States and the Wiandot and Delaware nations, shall begin at the mouth of the river Cayahoga, and run thence up the said river to the portage between that and the Tuscarawas branch of Meskingum; then down the said branch to the forks at the crossing place above Fort Lawrence; then westerly to the portage of the Big Miami, which runs into the Ohio, at the mouth of which branch the fort stood which was taken by the French in one thousand seven hundred and fifty-two; then along the said portage to the Great Miami or Ome river, and down the south-east side of the same to its mouth; thence along the south shore of lake Erie, to the mouth of Cayahoga where it began.

ARTICLE IV.

The United States allot all the lands contained within the said lines to the Wiandot and Delaware nations, to live and to hunt on, and to such of the Ottawa nation as now live thereon; saving and reserving for the establishment of trading posts, six miles square at the mouth of Miami or Ome river, and the same at the portage on that branch of the Big Miami which runs into the Ohio, and the same on the lake of Sanduske where the fort formerly stood, and also two miles square on each side of the lower rapids of Sanduske river, which posts and the lands annexed to them, shall be to the use and under the government of the United States.

ARTICLE V.

If any citizen of the United States, or other person not being an Indian, shall attempt to settle on any of the lands allotted to the Wiandot and Delaware nations in this treaty, except on the lands reserved to the United States in the preceding article, such person shall forfeit the protection of the United States, and the Indians may punish him as they please.

ARTICLE VI.

The Indians who sign this treaty, as well in behalf of all their tribes as of themselves, do acknowledge the lands east, south and west of the lines described in the third article, so far as the said Indians formerly claimed the same, to belong to the United States; and none of their tribes shall presume to settle upon the same, or any part of it.

ARTICLE VII.

The post of Detroit, with a district beginning at the mouth of the river Rosine, on the west end of lake Erie, and running west six miles up the southern bank of the said river, thence northerly and always six miles west of the strait, till it strikes the lake St. Clair, shall be also reserved to the sole use of the United States.

ARTICLE VIII.

In the same manner the post of Michillimachenac with its dependencies, and twelve miles square about the same, shall be reserved to the use of the United States.

ARTICLE IX

If any Indian or Indians shall commit a robbery or murder on any citizen of the United States, the tribe to which such offenders may belong, shall be bound to deliver them up at the nearest post, to be punished according to the ordinances of the United States.

ARTICLE X

The Commissioners of the United States, in pursuance of the humane and liberal views of Congress, upon this treaty's being signed, will direct goods to be distributed among the different tribes for their use and comfort.

SEPARATE ARTICLE.

It is agreed that the Delaware chiefs, Kelelamand or lieutenant-colonel Henry, Hengue Pushees or the Big Cat, Wicocalind or Captain White Eyes, who took up the hatchet for the United States, and their families, shall be received into the Delaware nation, in the same situation and rank as before the war, and enjoy their due portions of the lands given to the Wiandot and Delaware nations in this treaty, as fully as if they had not taken part with America, or as any other person or persons in the said nations.

Go. Clark

Richard Butler

Arthur Lee

Daunghquat, his x mark

Abraham Kuhn, his x mark

Ottawerreri, his x mark

Hobocan, his x mark

Walendightun, his x mark

Quecookkia, his x mark

Talapoxic, his x mark

Wingenum, his x mark

Packelant, his x mark

Gingewanno, his x mark

Waanoos, his x mark

Konalawassee his x mark

Shawnaquin, his x mark

Witness:

Sam'l J. Atlee

Fras. Johnston

I. Bradford

George Slaughter

Pennsylvania Commissioners.

Alex. Campbell

Jos. Harmar, lieutenant-colonel commandant

Alex. Lowrey

Joseph Nicholas, interpreter.

Van Swearingen

John Boggs

G. Evans

D. Luckett

1785 CE Nov. 28

Synopsis: **Treaty with The Cherokee**

Indians to restore all prisoners, etc. ; United States to restore all prisoners.

Cherokees acknowledge protection of United States. Boundaries. No citizens of United States to settle on Indian lands. Indians to deliver up criminals. Citizens of United States committing crimes against Indians to be punished. Retaliation prohibited. United States to regulate trade.

Special provision for trade. Indians to give notice of designs against United States. Indians may send deputy to Congress. Peace and friendship perpetual.

1786 CE

Treaty with the Choctaw *(Full Text)*

Articles of a treaty concluded at Hopewell, on the
Keowee, near Seneca Old Town, between Benjamin
Hawkins, Andrew Pickens and Joseph Martin,
Commissioners Plenipotentiary of the United States of
America, of the one part; and Yockonahoma, great
Medal Chief of Soonacoha; Yockehoopoie, leading Chief
of Bugtoogoloo; Mingohoopoie, leading Chief of
Hasooqua; Tobocoh, great Medal Chief of Congetoo;
Pooshemastubie, Gorget Captain of Senayazo; and
thirteen small Medal Chiefs of the first Class, twelve
Medal and Gorget Captains, Commissioners
Plenipotentiary of all the Choctaw Nation, of the other
part.

THE Commissioners Plenipotentiary of the United States
of America give peace to all the Choctaw nation, and
receive them into the favor and protection of the United
States of America, on the following conditions:

ARTICLE I.

The Commissioners Plenipotentiary of all the Choctaw nation, shall restore all the prisoners, citizens of the United States, or subjects of their allies, to their entire liberty, if any there be in the Choctaw nation.

They shall also restore all the negroes, and all other property taken during the late war, from the citizens. to such person, and at such time and place as the Commissioners of the United States of America shall appoint, if any there be in the Choctaw nation.

ARTICLE II.

The Commissioners Plenipotentiary of all the Choctaw nation, do hereby acknowledge the tribes and towns of the said nation, and the lands within the boundary allotted to the said Indians to live and hunt on, as mentioned in the third article, to be under the protection of the United States of America, and of no other sovereign whosoever.

ARTICLE III.

The boundary of the lands hereby allotted to the Choctaw nation to live and hunt on, within the limits of the United States of America, is and shall be the following, viz.

Beginning at a point on the thirty-first degree of north latitude, where the Eastern boundary of the Natches district shall touch the same; thence east along the said thirty-first degree of north latitude, being the southern boundary of the United States of America, until it shall strike the eastern boundary of the lands on which the Indians of the said nation did live and hunt on the twenty-ninth of November, one thousand seven hundred and eighty-two, while they were under the protection of the King of Great-Britain; thence northerly along the said eastern boundary, until it shall meet the northern boundary of the said lands; thence westerly along the said northern boundary, until it shall meet the western boundary thereof; thence southerly along the same to the beginning: saving and reserving for the establishment of trading posts, three tracts or parcels of land of six miles square each, at such places as the United [States] in Congress assembled shall think proper; which posts, and the lands annexed to them, shall be to the use and under the government of the United States of America.

ARTICLE IV.

If any citizen of the United States, or other person not being an Indian, shall attempt to settle on any of the lands hereby allotted to the Indians to live and hunt on, such person shall forfeit the protection of the United States of America, and the Indians may punish him or not as they please.

ARTICLE V.

If any Indian or Indians, or persons, residing among them. or who shall take refuge in their nation, shall commit a robbery or murder or other capital crime on any citizen of the United States of America, or person under their protection, the tribe to which such offender may belong, or the nation, shall be bound to deliver him or them up to be punished according to the ordinances of the United States in Congress assembled: Provided, that the punishment shall not be greater than if the robbery or murder, or other capital crime, had been committed by a citizen on a citizen.

ARTICLE VI.

If any citizen of the United States of America, or person under their protection, shall commit a robbery or murder, or other capital crime, on any Indian, such offender or offenders shall be punished in the same manner as if the robbery or murder, or other capital crime, had been committed on a citizen of the United States of America; and the punishment shall be in presence of some of the Choctaws, if any will attend at the time and place; and that they may have an opportunity so to do, due notice, if practicable, of the time of such intended punishment, shall be sent to some one of the tribes.

ARTICLE VII.

It is understood that the punishment of the innocent, under the idea of retaliation, is unjust, and shall not be practiced on either side, except where there is a manifest violation of this treaty; and then it shall be preceded, first by a demand of justice, and if refused, then by a declaration of hostilities.

ARTICLE VIII.

For the benefit and comfort of the Indians, and for the prevention of injuries or oppressions on the part of the citizens or Indians, the United States in Congress assembled, shall have the sole and exclusive right of regulating the trade with the Indians, and managing all their affairs in such manner as they think proper.

ARTICLE IX.

Until the pleasure of Congress be known, respecting the eighth article, all traders, citizens of the United States of

America, shall have liberty to go to any of the tribes or towns of the Choctaws, to trade with them, and they shall be protected in their persons and property, and kindly treated.

ARTICLE X.

The said Indians shall give notice to the citizens of the United States of America, of any designs which they may know or suspect to be formed in any neighboring tribe, or by any person whosoever, against the peace, trade or interest of the United States of America.

ARTICLE XI.

The hatchet shall be forever buried, and the peace given by the United States of America, and friendship re-established between the said states on the one part, and all the Choctaw nation on the other part, shall be universal; and the contracting parties shall use their utmost endeavors to maintain the peace given as aforesaid, and friendship re-established.

In witness of all and every thing herein determined, between the United States of America and all the Choctaws, we, their underwritten commissioners, by virtue of our full powers, have signed this definitive treaty, and have caused our seals to be hereunto affixed.

Done at Hopewell, on the Keowee, this third day of January, in the year of our Lord one thousand seven hundred and eighty-six.

Benjamin Hawkins,
Andrew Pickens,
Jos. Martin,
Yockenahoma, his x mark,
Yorkehoopoie, his x mark,
Mingohoopole, his x mark,
Tobocoh, his x mark,
Pooshemastuby, his x mark
Pooshahooma, his x mark,
Tuseoonoohoopoie, his x mark,
Shinshemastuby, his x mark
Yoopahooma, his x mark

Stoonokoohoopoie, his x mark,
Tehakuhbay, his x mark,
Pooshernastuby, his x mark,
Tuskkahoommh, his x mark,
Yoostenochla his x mark,
Tootehooma, his x mark,
Toobenohoomoch. his x mark.
Cshecoopoohcomoch, his x mark,
Stonakoohoopoie, his x mark
Tushkoheegohta, his x mark
Teshuhenoehloeh, his x mark,
Pooshonaltla, his x mark,
Okaneonnooba, his x mark,
Autoonachuba, his x mark
Pangehooloch, his x mark,
Steabee, his x mark,
Tenetchenna, his x mark,
Tushkementahock, his x mark,
Tushtallay, his x mark,
Cshnaangehabba, his x mark,
Cunnopoie, his x mark,
Witness:
Wm. Blount,

John Woods,

Saml. Tavlor,

Robert Anderson,

Benj. Lawrence.

John Pitchlynn,

James Cole,

Interpreters.

1786 CE

Treaty with the Chickasaw.

Articles of a treaty, concluded at Hopewell, on the Keowee, near Seneca Old Town, Between Benjamin Hawkins, Andrew Pickens and Joseph Martin, Commissioners Plenipotentiary of the United States of America, of the one Part; and Piomingo, Head Warrior and First Minister of the Chickasaw Nation; Mingatushka, one of the leading Chiefs; and Latopoia, first beloved Man of the said Nation, Commissioners Plenipotentiary of all the Chickasaws, of the other Part.

THE Commissioners Plenipotentiary of the United States of America give peace to the Chickasaw Nation, and receive them into the favor and protection of the said States, on the following conditions:

ARTICLE I.

The Commissioners Plenipotentiary of the Chickasaw nation, shall restore all the prisoners, citizens of the United States, to their entire liberty, if any there be in the Chickasaw nation.

They shall also restore all the negroes, and all other property taken during the late war, from the citizens, if any there be in the Chickasaw nation, to such person, and at such time and place, as the Commissioners of the United States of America shall appoint.

ARTICLE II.

The Commissioners Plenipotentiary of the Chickasaws, do hereby acknowledge the tribes and the towns of the

Chickasaw nation, to be under the protection of the United States of America, and of no other sovereign whosoever.

ARTICLE III.

The boundary of the lands hereby allotted to the Chickasaw nation to live and hunt on, within the limits of the United States of America, is, and shall be the following, viz. Beginning on the ridge that divides the waters running into the Cumberland, from those running into the Tennessee, at a point in a line to be run north-east, which shall strike the Tennessee at the mouth of Duck river; thence running westerly along the said ridge, till it shall strike the Ohio; thence down the southern banks thereof to the Mississippi; thence down the same, to the Choctaw line or Natches district; thence along the said line, or the line of the district eastwardly as far as the Chickasaws claimed, and lived and hunted on, the twenty-ninth of November, one thousand seven hundred and eighty-two. Thence the said boundary, eastwardly, shall be the lands allotted to the Choctaws and Cherokees to live and hunt on, and the lands at present in the possession of the Creeks; saving and reserving for the establishment of a trading post, a tract or parcel of land to be laid out at the lower port of the Muscle shoals, at the mouth of Ocochappo, in a circle, the diameter of which shall be five miles on the river, which post, and the lands annexed thereto, shall be to the use and under the government of the United States of America.

ARTICLE IV.

If any citizen of the United States, or other person not being an Indian, shall attempt to settle on any of the lands hereby allotted to i the Chickasaws to live and hunt on, such person shall forfeit the protection of the United States of America, and the Chickasaws may punish him or not as they please.

ARTICLE V.

If any Indian or Indians, or persons residing among them, or who shall take refuge in their nation, shall commit a robbery or murder, or other capital crime, on any citizen of the United States, or person under their protection, the tribe to which such offender or offenders may belong, or the nation, shall be bound to deliver him or them up to be punished according to the ordinances of the United States in Congress assembled: Provided, that the punishment shall not be greater, than if the robbery or murder, or other capital crime, had been committed by a citizen on a citizen.

ARTICLE VI.

If any citizen of the United States of America, or person under their protection, shall commit a robbery or murder, or other capital crime, on any Indian, such offender or offenders shall be punished in the same manner as if the robbery or murder or other capital crime had been committed on a citizen of the United States of America; and the punishment shall be in presence of some of the Chickasaws, if any will attend at the time and place, and that they may have an opportunity so to do, due notice, if practicable, of such intended punishment, shall be sent to some one of the tribes.

ARTICLE VII.

It is understood that the punishment of the innocent under the idea of retaliation is unjust, and shall not be practiced on either side, except where there is a manifest violation of this treaty; and then it shall be preceded, first by a demand of justice, and if refused, then by a declaration of hostilities.

ARTICLE VIII.

For the benefit and comfort of the Indians, and for the prevention of injuries or oppressions on the part of the citizens or Indians, the United States in Congress assembled shall have the sole and exclusive right of regulating the trade with the Indians, and managing all their affairs in such manner as they think proper.

ARTICLE IX.

Until the pleasure of Congress be known respecting the eighth article, all traders, citizens of the United States, shall have liberty to go to any of the tribes or towns of the Chickasaws to trade with them, and they shall be protected in their persons and property, and kindly treated.

ARTICLE X.

The said Indians shall give notice to the citizens of the United States of America, of any designs which they may know or suspect. to be formed in any neighboring tribe, or by any person whosoever, against the peace, trade or interests of the United States of America.

ARTICLE XI.

The hatchet shall he forever buried, and the peace given by the United States of America, and friendship re-established between the said States on the one part, and the Chickasaw nation on the other part, shall be universe: and the contracting parties shall use their utmost endeavors to maintain the peace given as aforesaid, and friendship re-established.

In witness of all and every thing herein contained, between the said States and Chickasaws, we, their underwritten commissioners, by virtue of our full powers, have signed this definitive treaty, and have caused our seals to he hereunto affixed.

Done at Hopewell, on the Keowee, this tenth day of January, in the year of our Lord one thousand seven hundred and eighty-six.

Benjamin Hawkins,
And'w. Pickens,
Jos. Martin,
Piomingo, his x mark,
Mingatushka, his x mark,
Latopoia, his x mark,

Witness:
Wm. Blount,

Wm. Hazard,

Sam. Taylor,

James Cole,

Sworn Interpreter.

1786 CE

Treaty with the Shawnee

Articles of a Treaty concluded at the Mouth of the Great
Miami, on the North-western Bank of the Ohio, the
thirty-first day of January, one thousand seven hundred
arid eighty-six, between the Commissioners
Plenipotentiary of the United States of America, of the
one Part, and the Chiefs and Warriors of the Shawnoe
Nation, of the other Part.

ARTICLE 1.

THREE hostages shall be immediately delivered to the
Commissioners, to remain in the possession of the
United States until all the prisoners, white and black,
taken in the late war from among the citizens of the
United States,

by the Shawanoe nation, or by any other Indian or Indians residing in their towns, shall be restored.

ARTICLE II.

The Shawanoe nation do acknowledge the United States to be the sole and absolute sovereigns of all the territory ceded to them by treaty of peace, made between them and the King of Great Britain the fourteenth day of January, one thousand seven hundred and eighty-four.

ARTICLE III.

If any Indian or Indians of the Shawanoe nation, or any other Indian or Indians residing in their towns, shall commit murder or robbery on, or do any injury to the citizens of the United States, or any of them, that nation shall deliver such offender or offenders to the officer commending the nearest post of the United States, to be punished according to the ordinances of Congress; and in like manner, any citizen of the United States, who shall do an injury to any Indian of the Shawanoe nation, or to any other Indian or Indians residing in their towns, and under their protection, shall be punished according to the laws of the United States.

ARTICLE IV.

The Shawanoe nation having knowledge of the intention of any nation or body of Indians to make war on the citizens of the United States, or of their counselling together for that purpose, and neglecting to give information thereof to the commanding officer of the nearest post of the United States, shall be considered as parties in such war and be punished accordingly: and the United States shall in like manner inform the Shawanoes of any injury designed against them.

ARTICLE V.

The United States do grant peace to the Shawanoe nation, and do receive them into their friendship and protection.

ARTICLE VI.

The United Sates do allot to the Shawanoe nation, lands within their territory to live and hunt upon, beginning at the south line of the lands allotted to the Wiandots and Delaware nations, at the place where the main branch of the Great Miami, which falls into the Ohio, intersects said line; then down the river Miami, to the fork of that river, next below the old fort which was taken by the French in one thousand seven hundred and fifty-two; thence due west to the river de la Panse; then down that river to the river Wabash, beyond which lines none of the citizens of the United States shall settle, nor disturb the Shawanoes in their settlement and possessions; and the Shawanoes do relinquish to the United States, all title, or presence of title, they ever had to the lands east, west and south, of the east, west and south lines before described.

ARTICLE VII.

If any citizen or citizens of the United States, shall presume to settle upon the lands allotted to the Shawanoes by this treaty, he or they shall be put out of the protection of the United States.

On testimony whereof, the parties hereunto have affixed their hands

G. Clark
Richard Butler,
Samuel H. Parsons,
Aweecony, his x mark
Kakawipilathy, his x mark,
Malunthy. his x mark.
Musquaconocah, his x mark
Meanymsecah, his x mark,
Waupaucowela, his x mark,
Nihipeewa, his x mark
Nihinessicoe' his x mark,

Attest:

Alexander Campbell, Secretary Commissioners

Witnesses:

W. Finney, Maj. B. B.

Thos. Doyle, Capt. B. B.

Nathan MeDowell, Ensign

John Saffenger,

Henry Govy,

Kagy Galloway, his x mark,

John Boggs

Samuel Montgomery

Daniel Elliott

James Rinker,

Nathaniel Smith,

Joseph Suffrein, his x mark, or Kemepemo Shawno,

Isaac Zane, (Wyandot) his x mark,

The Half King of the Wyandots,

The Crane of the Wyandots, their x mark,

Capt. Pipe, of the Delawares, his x mark,

Capt. Bohongehelas, his x mark

Tetebockshicka, his x mark,

The Big Cat of the Delawares, his x mark

Pierre Droullar.

1789 CE

Treaty with the Wyandot, etc.,

Articles of a Treaty Made at Fort Harmar, between Arthur St. Clair, Governor of the Territory of the United States North-West of the River Ohio, and Commissioner Plenipotentiary of the United States of America, for removing all Causes of Controversy, regulating Trade, and settling Boundaries, with the India Nations in the Northern Department, of the one Part; and the Sachems and Warriors of the Wiandot, Delaware, Ottawa, Chippewa, Pattawatima and Sac Naions, on the other Part.

ARTICLE I.

WHEREAS the United States in Congress assembled, did, by their Commissioners George Rogers Clark, Richard Butler, and Arthur Lee, Esquires, duly appointed for that purpose, at a treaty holden with the Wiandot, Delaware, Ottawa and Chippewa nations, at Fort M'lntosh, on the twenty-first day of January, in the year of our Lord one thousand seven hundred and eighty-five, conclude a peace with the Wyandots, Delawares, Ottawas and Chippewas, and take them into their friendship and protection: And whereas at the said treaty it was stipulated that all prisoners that had been made by those nations, or either of them, should be delivered up to the United States. And whereas the said nations have now agreed to and with the aforesaid Arthur St. Clair, to renew and confirm all the engagements they had made with the United States of America. at the before mentioned treaty except so far as are altered by these presents. And there are now in the possession of some individuals of these nations, certain prisoners, who have been taken by others not in peace with the said United States, or in violation of the treaties subsisting between the United States and them; the said nations agree to deliver up all the prisoners now in their hands (by what means soever they may have come into their possession) to the said Governor St. Clair, at Fort Harmar, or in his absence, to the officer commanding there, as soon as conveniently may be; and for the true performance of this agreement, they do now agree to deliver into his hands, two persons of the Wyandot Nation, to be retained in the hands of the United States as hostages, until the said prisoners are restored; after which they shall be sent back to their nation.

ARTICLE II.

And whereas at the before mentioned treaty it was agreed between the United States and said nations, that a boundary line should be fixed between the lands of those nations and the territory of the United States; which boundary is as follows, viz.-Beginning at the mouth of Cayahoga river, and running thence up the said river to the portage between that and the

Tuscarawa branch of Muskingum, then down the said branch to the forks at the crossing-place above fort Lawrence, thence westerly to the portage on that branch of the Big Miami river which runs into the Ohio, at the mouth of which branch the fort stood which was taken by the French in the year of our Lord one thousand seven hundred and fifty-two, then along the said portage to the Great Miami or Omie river, and down the south-east side of the same to its mouth; thence along the southern shore of Lake Erie to the mouth of Cayahoga, where it began. And the said Wyandot, Delaware, Ottawa and Chippewa Nations, for and in consideration of the peace then granted to them by the said United States, and the presents they then received, as well as of a quantity of goods to the value of six thousand dollars, now delivered to them by the said Arthur St. Clair, the receipt whereof they do hereby acknowledge, do by these presents renew and confirm the said boundary line; to the end that the same may remain as a division line between the lands of the United States of America, and the lands of said nations, forever. And the undersigned Indians do hereby in their own names and the names of their respective nations and tribes, their heirs and descendants, for the consideration above-mentioned, release, quit claim, relinquish and cede to the said United States, all the land east, south and west of the lines above described, so far as the said Indians formerly claimed the same; for them the said United States to have and to hold the same in true and absolute propriety forever.

ARTICLE III.

The United States of America do by these presents relinquish and quit claim to the said nations respectively, all the lands lying between the limits above described, for them the said Indians to live and hunt upon, and otherwise to occupy as they shall see fit: But the said nations or either of them, shall not be at liberty to sell or dispose of the same, or any part thereof, to any sovereign power, except the United States; nor to the subjects or citizens of any other sovereign power, nor to the subjects or citizens of the United States.

ARTICLE IV.

It is agreed between the said United States and the said nations, that the individuals of said nations shall be at liberty to hunt within the territory ceded to the United States, without hindrance or molestation, so long as they demean themselves peaceably, and offer no injury or annoyance to any of the subjects or citizens of the said United States.

ARTICLE V.

It is agreed that if any Indian or Indians of the nations before mentioned, shall commit a murder or robbery on any of the citizens of the United States, the nation or tribe to which the offende belongs, on complaint being made, shall deliver up the person or persons complained of, at the nearest post of the United States; to the end that he or they may be tried, and if found guilty, punished according to the laws established in the territory of the United States north-west of the river Ohio, for the punishment of such offences, if the same shall have been committed within the said territory; or according to the laws of the State where the offence may have been committed, if the same has happened in any of the United States. In like manner, if any subject or citizen of the United States shall commit murder or robbery on any Indian or Indians of the said nations, upon complaint being made thereof, he or they shall be arrested, tried and punished agreeable to the laws of the state or of the wherein the offence was committed; that nothing may interrupt the peace and harmony now established between the United States and said nations.

ARTICLE VI.

And whereas the practice of stealing horses has prevailed very much, to the great disquiet of the citizens of the United States, and if persisted in, cannot fail to involve both the United States of America and the Indians in endless animosity, it is agreed that it shall be put an entire stop to on both sides; nevertheless, should some individuals, in defiance of this agreement, and of the laws provided against such offences, continue to make depredations of that nature, the person convicted thereof shall be punished with the utmost severity the laws of the respective states, or territory of the United States north-west of the Ohio, where the offence may have been committed, will admit of: And all horses so stolen, either by the Indians from the citizens or subjects of the United States, or by the citizens or subjects of the United States from any of the Indian nations, may be reclaimed, into whose possession soever they may have passed, and, upon due proof, shall be restored; any sales in market overt. notwithstanding. And the civil magistrates in the United States respectively, and in the territory of the United States north-west of the Ohio, shall give all necessary aid and protection to Indians claiming such stolen horses.

ARTICLE VII.

Trade shall be opened with the said nations, and they do hereby respectively engage to afford protection to the persons and property oft such as may be duly licensed to reside among them I or the purposes of trade, and to their agents, factors and servants; but no person shall be permitted to reside at their towns, or at their hunting camps, as a trader, who is not furnished with a license for that purpose, under the hand and seal of the Governor of the territory of the United States north-west of the Ohio, for the time being, or under the hand and seal of one of his deputies for the management of Indian affairs; to the end that they may not be imposed upon in their traffic. And if any person or persons shall intrude themselves without such licence; they promise to apprehend him or them, and to bring them to the said Governor, or one of his deputies, for the purpose before mentioned, to be dealt with according to law: And that they may be defended against persons who might attempt to forge such licenses, they further engage to give information to the said Governor, or one of his deputies, of the names of all traders residing among them from time to time, and at least once in every year.

ARTICLE VIII.

Should any nation of Indians meditate a war against the United States, or either of them, and the same shall come to the knowledge of the before mentioned nations, or either of them, they do hereby engage to give immediate notice thereof to the Governor, or in his absence to the officer commanding the troops of the United States at the nearest post. And should any nation with hostile intentions against the United States, or either of them, attempt to pass through their country, they will endeavor to prevent the same, and in like manner give information of such attempt to the said Governor or commanding officer, as soon as possible, that all causes of mistrust and suspicion may be avoided between them and the United States: In like manner the United States shall give notice to the said Indian nations, of any harm that may be meditated against them, or either of them, that shall come to their knowledge; and do all in their power to hinder and prevent the same, that the friendship between them may be uninterrupted.

ARTICLE IX.

If any person or persons, citizens or subjects of the United States, or any other person not being an Indian, shall presume to settle upon the lands confirmed to the said nations, he and they shall be out of the protection of the United States; and the said nations may punish him or them in such manner as they see fit.

ARTICLE X.

The United States renew the reservations heretofore made in the before mentioned treaty at Fort M'lntosh, for the establishment of trading posts, in manner and form following; that is to say: Six miles square at the mouth of the Miami or Omie river; six miles square at the portage upon that branch of the Miami which runs into the Ohio; six miles square upon the lake Sandusky where the fort formerly stood; and two miles square upon each side the Lower Rapids on Sandusky river, which posts, and the lands annexed to them, shall be for the use and under the government of the United States.

ARTICLE XI.

The post at Detroit, with a district of land beginning at the mouth of the river Rosine, at the west end of lake Erie, and running up the southern bank of said river six miles; thence northerly, and always six miles west of the strait. until it strikes the lake St. Clair, shall be reserved for the use of the United States.

ARTICLE XII.

In like manner the post at Michilimackinac, with its dependencies, and twelve miles square about the same, shall be reserved to the sole use of the United States.

ARTICLE XIII.

The United States of America do hereby renew and confirm the peace and friendship entered into with the said nations, at the treaty before mentioned, held at Fort M'Intosh; and the said nations again acknowledge themselves, and all their tribes, to be under the protection of the said United States, and no other power whatever.

ARTICLE XIV.

The United States of America do also receive into their friendship and protection, the nations of the Pattiwatimas and Sacs; and do hereby establish a league of peace and amity between them respectively; and all the articles of this treaty, so far as they apply to these nations, are to be considered as made and concluded in all, and every part, expressly with them and each of them.

ARTICLE XV.

And whereas in describing the boundary before mentioned, the words, if strictly constructed, would carry it from the portage on that branch of the Miami, which runs into the Ohio, over to the river Au Glaize; which was neither the intention of the Indians, nor of the Commissioners; it is hereby declared, that the line shall run from the said portage directly to the first fork of the Miami river, which is to the southward and eastward of the Miami village, thence down the main branch of the Miami river to the said village, and thence down that river to Lake Erie, and along the- margin of the lake to the place of beginning.

Done at Fort Harmar, on the Muskingum, this ninth day of January, in the year of our Lord one thousand seven hundred and eighty nine.

In witness whereof, the parties have hereunto interchangeably set their hands and seals.

Arthur St. Clair,
Peoutewatamie, his x mark,
Konatikina, his x mark,

Sacs:
Tepakee, his x mark
Kesheylva, his x: mark,

Chippewas:

Mesass, his x mark

Paushquash, his x mark,

Pawasicko, his x mark,

Ottawas:

Wewiskia, his x mark,

Neagey, his x mark,

Pattawatimas:

Windigo, his x mark,

Wapaskea, his x mark,

Nequea, his x mark,

Delawares:

Captain Pipe, his x mark,

Wingenond, his x mark

Pekelan, his x mark,

Teataway, his x mark,

Chippewas:

Nanamakeak, his x mark

Wetenasa, his x mark,

Soskene, his x mark,

Pewanakum, his x mark,

Wyandots:

Teyandatontec, his x mark

Cheyawe, his x mark,

Doueyenteat, his x mark

Tarhe, his x mark,

Terhataw, his x mark,

Datasay, his x mark

Maudoronk, his x mark,

Skahomat, his x mark,

In presence of-

Jos. Harmar, lieutenant-colonel, eommandant, First U. S. Regiment, and brigadier-general by brevet,

Richard Butler,

Jno. Gibson

Will. McCurdey, captain

E. Denny, ensign, First U. S. Regiment,

F. A. Hartshorn. ensign.

Robt. Thompson, ensign, First U. S. Regiment,

Frans. Muse, ensign J. Williams, jr.,

Wm. Wilson,

Joseph Nicholas James Rinkin.

Be it remembered, That the Wyandots have laid claim to the lands that were granted to the Shawanese, at the treaty held at the Miami, and have declared, that as the Shawanese have been so restless, and caused so much trouble, both to them and to the United States, if they will not now be at peace, they will dispossess them, and take the country into their own hands; for that the country is theirs of right, and the Shawanese are only living upon it by their permission. They further lay claim to all the country west of the Miami boundary, from the village to the lake Erie, and declare that it is now under their management and direction.

SEPARATE ARTICLE.

Whereas the Wyandots have represented, that within the reservation from the river Rosine along the Strait, they have two villages from which they cannot with any convenience remove; it is agreed, that they shall remain in possession of the same, and shall not be in any manner disturbed therein.

SEPARATE ARTICLE.

Should a robbery or murder be committed by an Indian or Indians of the said nations upon the citizens or subjects of the United States or

any of them, or by the citizens or subjects of the United States or any of them, upon any Indian or Indians of the said nations, the parties accused of the same shall be tried, and, if found guilty, be punished according to the laws of the state, or of the territory of the United States, as the case may be, where the same was committed; and should any horses be stolen, either by the Indians of the said nations from the citizens or subjects of the United States or any of them, or by any of the said citizens and subjects from any of the said Indians, they may be reclaimed, into whose possession soever they may have come; and, upon due proof, shall be restored, any sales in open market notwithstanding. And the parties convicted shall be punished with the utmost severity the laws will admit; and the said nations engage to deliver the parties that may be accused of their nations of either of the before-mentioned crimes, at the nearest post of the United States, if the crime was committed within the territory of the United States, or to the civil authority of the States, if it shall have happened within any of the United States.

1789 CE

Treaty with the Six Nations

Articles of a treaty made at Fort Harmar, the ninth day of January, in the year of our Lord one thousand seven hundred and eighty-nine, between Arthur St. Clair, esquire, Governor of the territory of the United States of America, northwest of the river Ohio, and Commissioner plenipotentiary of the said United States, for removing all causes of controversy, regulating trade, arid settling boundaries, between the Indian nations in the northerly department and the said United States, of the one part, and the sachems and warriors of the Six Nations, of the other part:

ART. 1.

WHEREAS the United States, in congress assembled, did, by their commissioners, Oliver Wolcott, Richard Butler, and Arthur Lee, esquires, duly appointed for that purpose, at a treaty held with the said Six Nations, viz: with the Mohawks, Oneidas, Onondagas, Tuscaroras, Cayugas, and Senekas, at fort Stanwix, on the twenty-second day of October, one thousand seven hundred and eighty-four, give peace to the said nations, and receive them into their friendship and protection: And whereas the said nations have now agreed to and with the said Arthur St. Clair, to renew and confirm all the engagements and stipulations entered into at the before mentioned treaty at fort Stanwix: and whereas it was then and there agreed, between the United States of America and the said Six Nations, that a boundary line should be fixed between the lands of the said Six

Nations and the territory of the said United States, which boundary line is as follows, viz: Beginning at the mouth of a creek, about four miles east of Niagara, called Ononwayea, or Johnston's Landing Place, upon the lake named by the Indians Oswego, and by us Ontario; from thence southerly, in a direction always four miles east of the carrying place, between lake Erie and lake Ontario, to the mouth of Tehoseroton, or Buffalo creek, upon lake Erie; thence south, to the northern boundary of the state of Pennsylvania; thence west, to the end of the said north boundary; thence south, along the west boundary of the said state to the river Ohio. The said line, from the mouth of Ononwayea to the Ohio, shall be the western boundary of the lands of the Six Nations, so that the Six Nations shall and do yield to the United States, all claim to the country west of the said boundary; and then they shall be secured in the possession of the lands they inhabit east, north, and south of the safne, reserving only six miles square, round the fort of Oswego, for the support of the same.

The said Six Nations, except the Mohawks none of whom have attended at this time, for and in consideration of the peace then granted to them, the presents they then received, as well as in consideration of a quantity of goods, to the value of three thousand dollars, now delivered to them by the said Arthur St. Clair, the receipt whereof they do hereby acknowledge, do hereby renew and confirm the said boundary line in the words beforementioned, to the end that it may be and remain as a division line between the lands of the said Six Nations and the territory of the United States, forever. And the undersigned Indians, as well in their own names as in the name of their respective tribes and nations, their heirs and descendants, for the considerations beforementioned, do release, quit claim, relinquish, and cede, to the United States of America, all the lands west of the said boundary or division line, and between the said line and the strait, from the mouth of Ononwayea and Buffalo Creek, for them, the said United States of America, to have and to hold the same, in true and absolute propriety, forever.

ART. 2.

The United States of America confirm to the Six Nations all the lands which they inhabit, lying east and north of the beforementioned boundary line, and relinquish and quit claim to the same and every part thereof, excepting only six miles square round the fort of Oswego, which six miles square round said fort is again reserved to the United States by these presents.

ART. 3.

The Oneida and Tuscarora nations, are also again secured and confirmed in the possession of their respective lands.

ART. 4.

The United States of America renew and confirm the peace and friendship entered into with the Six Nations, (except the Mohawks) at the treaty beforementioned, held at fort Stanwix, declaring the same to be perpetual.

And if the Mohawks shall, within six months, declare their assent to the same, they shall be considered as included.

Done at Harmar, on the Muskingum, the day and year first above written.

In witness whereof, the parties have hereunto, interchangeably, set their hands and seals.

Ar. St. Clair,

Cageaga, or Dogs Round the Fire,

Sawedowa, or The Blast,

Kiondushowa, or Swimming Fish,

Oneahye, or Lancing Feather

Sohaeas, or Falling Mountain,

Otachsaka, or Broken Tomahawk, his x mark,

Tekahias, or Long Tree, his x mark,

Oneensetee, or Loaded Man, his x mark,

Kiahtulaho, or Snake Aqueia, or Bandy Legs

Kiandogewa, or Big Tree, his x mark,

Owenewa, or Thrown in the Water his x mark

Gyantwaia, or Corn planter, his x mark,

Gyasota, or Big Cross, his x mark,

Kannassee, or New Arrow,

Achiout, or Half Town,

Anachout, orTheWasp, his x mark,

Chishekoa, or Wood Bug, his x mark,

Sessewa, or Big Bale of a Kettle,

Sciahowa, or Council Keeper,

Tewanias, or Broken Twig

Sonachshowa, or Full Moon

CachunwasÂ£e, or Twenty Canoes

Hickonquash, or Tearing asunder,

In presence of-
Jos. Harmar, lieutenant-colonel commanding First
Regiment and brigadier-general by brevet,
Richard Butler,
Jno. Gibson,
Will. M'Curdy, captain,
Ed. Denny, ensign First U. S. Regiment,
A. Hartshorn, ensign,
Robt. Thompson, ensign, First U. S. Regiment,
Fran. Belle, ensign,
Joseph Nicholas.

SEPARATE ARTICLE.

Should a robbery or murder be committed by an Indian or Indians of the Six Nations, upon the citizens or subjects of the United States, or by the citizens or subjects of the United States, or any of them, upon any of the Indians of the said nations, the parties accused of the same shall be tried, and if found guilty, be punished according to the laws of the state, or of the territory of the United States, as the case may be, where the same was committed. And should any horses be stolen, either by the Indians of the said nations, from the citizens or subjects of the United States, or any of them, or by any of the said citizens or subjects from any of the said Indians, they may be reclaimed mto whose possession soever they may have come; and, upon due proof, shall be restored, any sale in open market notwithstanding; and the persons convicted shall be punished with the utmost severity the laws will admit. And the said nations engage to deliver the persons that may be accused, of their nations, of either of the beforementioned crimes, at the nearest post of the United States, if the crime was committed within the territory of the United States; or to the civil authority of the state, ire it shall have happened within any of the United States.

Ar. St. Clair.

1790 CE

Treaty with the Creeks

A Treaty of Peace and Friendship made and concluded between the President of the United States of America, on the Part and Behalf of the said States, and the undersigned Kings, Chiefs, and Warriors of the Creek Nation of Indians, or the Part and Behalf of the said Nation.

THE parties being desirous of establishing permanent peace and friendship between the United States and the said Creek Nation, and the citizens and members thereof, and to remove the causes of war by ascertaining their limits, and making other necessary, just and friendly arrangements: The President of the United

States, by Henry Knox, Secretary for the Department of War, whom he hath constituted with full powers for these purposes, by and with the advice and consent of the Senate of the United States, and the Creek Nation, by the undersigned Kings, Chiefs and Warriors, representing the said nation, have agreed to the following articles.

ARTICLE I.

There shall be perpetual peace and friendship between all the citizens of the United States of America, and all the individuals, towns and tribes of the Upper, Middle and Lower Creeks and Semanolies composing the Creek nation of Indians.

ARTICLE II.

The undersigned Kings, Chiefs and Warriors, for themselves and all parts of the Creek Nation within the limits of the United States, do acknowledge themselves, and the said parts of the Creek nation, to be under the protection of the United States of America, and of no other sovereign whosoever; and they also stipulate that the said Creek Nation will not hold any treaty with an individual State, or with individuals of any State.

ARTICLE III.

The Creek Nation shall deliver as soon as practicable to the commanding officer of the troops of the United States, stationed at the Rock-Landing on the Oconee river, all citizens of the United States, white inhabitants or negroes, who are now prisoners in any part of the said nation. And if any such prisoners or negroes should not be so delivered, on or before the first day of June ensuing, the governor of Georgia may empower three persons to repair to the said nation, in order to claim and receive such prisoners and negroes.

ARTICLE IV.

The boundary between the citizens of the United States and the Creek Nation is, and shall be, from where the old line strikes the river Savannah; thence up the said river to a place on the most northern branch of the same, commonly called the Keowee, where a north east line to be drawn from the top of the Occunna mountain shall intersect; thence along the said line in a south-west direction to Tupelo river; thence to the top of the Currahee mountain; thence to the head or source of the main south branch of the Oconee river, called the Appalachee; thence down the middle of the said main south branch and river Oconee, to its confluence with the Oakmulgee, which form the river Altamaha; and thence down the middle of the said Altamaha to the old line on the said river, and thence along the said old line to the river St. Mary's.

And in order to preclude forever all disputes relatively to the head or source of the main south branch of the river Oconee, at the place where it shall be intersected by the line aforesaid, from the Currahee mountain, the same shall be ascertained by an able surveyor on the part of the United States, who shall be assisted by three old citizens of Georgia, who may be appointed by the Governor of the said state, and three old Creek chiefs, to be appointed by the said nation; and the said surveyor, citizens and chiefs shall assemble for this purpose, on the first day of October, one thousand one hundred and ninety-one, at the Rock Landing on the said rigor Oconee, and thence proceed to ascertain the said head or source of the main south branch of the said river, at the place where It shall be intersected by the line aforesaid, to be drawn from the Currahee mountain. And in order that the said boundary shall be rendered distinct and well known, it shall be marked by a line of felled trees at least twenty feet wide, and the trees chopped on each side from the said Currahee mountain, to the head or source of the said main south branch of the Oconee river, and thence down the margin of the said main south branch and river Oconee for the distance of twenty miles, or as much farther as may be necessary to mark distinctly the said boundary. And in order to extinguish forever all claims of the Creek nation, or any part thereof, to any of the land lying to the northward and eastward of the boundary herein described, it is hereby agreed, in addition to the considerations heretofore made for the said land, that the United States will cause certain valuable Indian goods now in the state of Georgia, to be delivered to the said Creek nation; and the said United States will also cause the sum of one thousand and five hundred dollars to be paid annually to the said Creek nation. And the undersigned Kings, Chiefs and Warriors, do hereby for themselves and the whole Creek nation, their heirs and descendants, for the considerations above-mentioned, release, quit claim, relinquish and cede, all the land to the northward and eastward of the boundary herein described.

ARTICLE V.

The United States solemnly guarantee to the Creek Nation, all their lands within the limits of the United States to the westward and southward of the boundary described in the preceding article.

ARTICLE VI.

If any citizen of the United States, or other person not being an Indian, shall attempt to settle on any of the Creeks lands, such person shall forfeit the protection of the United States, and the Creeks may punish him or not, as they please.

ARTICLE VII.

No citizen or inhabitant of the United States shall attempt to hunt or destroy the game on the Creek lands: Nor shall any such citizen or inhabitant go into the Creek country, without a passport first obtained from the Governor of some one of the United States, or the officer of the troops of the United States commanding at the nearest military post on the frontiers, or such other person as the President of the United States may, from time to time, authorize to grant the same.

ARTICLE VIII.

If any Creek Indian or Indians, or person residing among them, or who shall take refuge in their nation, shall commit a robbery or murder, or other capital crime, on any of the citizens or inhabitants of the United States, the Creek nation, or town, or tribe to which such offender or offenders may belong, shall be bound to deliver him or them up, to be punished according to the laws of the United States.

ARTICLE IX.

If any citizen or inhabitant of the United States, or of either of the territorial districts of the United States, shall go into any town, settlement or territory belonging to the Creek nation of Indians, and shall there commit any crime upon, or trespass against the person or property of any peaceable and friendly Indian or Indians, which if committed within the jurisdiction of any state, or within the jurisdiction of either of the said districts, against a citizen or white inhabitant thereof, would be punishable by the laws of such state or district, such offender or offenders shall be subject to the same punishment, and shall be proceeded against in the same manner, as if the offence had been committed within the jurisdiction of the state or district to which he or they may belong, against a citizen or white inhabitant thereof.

ARTICLE X.

In cases of violence on the persons or property of the individuals of either party, neither retaliation nor reprisal shall be committed by the other, until satisfaction shall have been demanded of the party, of which the aggressor is, and shall have been refused.

ARTICLE XI.

The Creeks shall give notice to the citizens of the United States of any designs, which they may know or suspect to be formed in any neighboring tribe, or by any person whatever, against the peace and interests of the United States.

ARTICLE XII.

That the Creek nation may be led to a greater degree of civilization, and to become herdsmen and cultivators, instead of remaining in a state of hunters, the United States will from time to time furnish gratuitously the said nation with useful domestic animals and implements of husbandry. And further to assist the said nation in so desirable a pursuit, and at the same time to establish a certain mode of communication, the United States will send such, and so many persons to reside in said nation as they may judge proper, and not exceeding four in number, who shall qualify themselves to act as interpreters. These persons shall have lands assigned them by the Creeks for cultivation, for themselves and their successors in office; but they shall be precluded exercising any kind of traffic.

ARTICLE XIII.

All animosities for past grievances shall henceforth cease; and the contracting parties will carry the foregoing treaty into full execution, with all good faith and sincerity.

ARTICLE XIV.

This treaty shall take effect and be obligatory on the contracting parties, as soon as the same shall have been ratified by the President of the United States, with the advice and consent of the Senate of the United States.

In witness of all and every thing herein determined, between the United States of America, and the whole Creek nation, the parties have hereunto set their hands and seals, in the city of New York, within the United States, this seventh day of August, one thousand seven hundred and ninety.

In behalf of the United States:

H. Knox,
Secretary of War and sole Commissioner for treating with the Creek nation of Indians.

In behalf of themselves and the whole Creek nation of Indians:

Alexander McGillivray,

Cusetahs: Fuskatche Mico, or Birdtail King, his x mark,

Neathlock, or Second Man, his x mark,

Halletemalthle, or Blue Giver, his x mark,

Little Tallisee: Opay Mico, or the Singer, his x mark,

Totkeshajou, or Samoniac, his x mark,

Big Tallisee: Hopothe Mico, or Tallisee King, his x mark

Opototache, or Long Side, his x mark,

Tuckabatehy: Soholessee, or Young Second Man, his x mark

Oeheehajou, or Aleck Cornel, his x mark

Natehez: Chinabie, or the Great Natehez Warrior, his x mark,

Natsowachehee, or the Great Natehez Warrior's Brother, his x mark

Thakoteehee, or the Mole, his x mark,

Oquakahee, his x mark,

Cowetas: Tuskenaah, or Big Lieutenant, his x mark

Homatah, or Leader, his x mark,

Chirmabie, or Matthews, his x mark,

Juleetaulematha, or Dry Pine, his x mark Of the Broken Arrow:

Chawookly Mico, his x mark,

Coosades: Coosades Hopoy, or the Measurer, his x mark
Muthtee, the Misser, his x mark,
Stimafutchkee, or Good Humor his x mark;
Alabama Chief: Stilnaleeje, or Disputer, his x mark,
Oaksoys: Mumagechee, David Francis, his x mark,

Done in the presence of- Richard Morris, chief justice of
the State of New York,
Richard Varick, mayor of the city of New York,
Marinus Willet,
Thomas Lee Shippen, of Pennsylvania,
John Rutledge, jun'r
Joseph Allen Smith,
Henry Izard,
Joseph Cornell, interpreter, His x mark.

1790 CE

When American pioneers attempted to settle the
Northwest Territory following the Ordinance of 1787, the
Indians, aided by the British fought fiercely for their
homes.

The first United States army sent to break the Indian resistance was commanded by Gen. Josiah Harmar. It met defeat (1790) at the Miami Indian villages (present Fort Wayne).

Many of the Shawnee, Miami, and others, decided to fight this new threat to their villages and way of life. Between 1783 and 1790, up to 1,500 settlers perished.

The principle chief of the Indian coalition against the United States was the Miami Chief Michikinikwa or Little Turtle who, on one occasion in October 1790, in the Ft. Wayne area, inflicted 200 casualties on General Josiah Harmar's force that had been sent to subdue the Indians.

Harmar's army totaled 1,453 men; 320 regular soldiers and the balance a poorly trained militia.

They left Fort Washington (Cincinnati) on September 26, 1790, and headed north through present day Lebanon and Xenia.

After reaching the Piqua area and the Great Miami River, he marched north, passing Loramie's Station on Loramie Creek in Shelby County, Ohio, in his quest to confront Little Turtle's forces.

Harmar, and his officers, including Colonel Hardin, had numerous confrontations with the Indians in the region, and although Harmar boasted of victory on his return to Fort Washington, historians refer to his escapades as, 'Harmar's defeat.'

(The Indians had hoped for British assistance; when that was not forthcoming, the indigenous people were compelled to sign the Treaty of Greenville in 1795, which ceded modern-day Ohio and part of Indiana to the United States.)

1787 CE

The Northwest Ordinance officially organized the Northwest Territory for white settlement. American settlers began pouring into the region. Violence erupted as indigenous tribes resisted this encroachment, and so the administration of President George Washington sent armed expeditions into the area to put down native resistance. However, in the Northwest Indian War, a pan-tribal confederacy led by Blue Jacket (Shawnee), Little Turtle (Miami), Buckongahelas (Lenape), and Egushawa (Ottawa) crushed armies led by Generals Josiah Harmar and Arthur St. Clair. General St. Clair's defeat was the most severe loss ever inflicted upon an American army by Native Americans.

The Americans attempted to negotiate a settlement, but Blue Jacket and the Shawnee-led confederacy insisted on a boundary line the Americans found unacceptable, and so a new expedition led by General Anthony Wayne was dispatched. Wayne's army defeated the Indian confederacy at the Battle of Fallen Timbers in 1794.

1790 CE

The US Trade and Intercourse Act prohibited states from acquiring land from Indians without federal approval.

1790 CE March 1

A Census Act is passed by Congress.

The first census, finished on Aug. 1, indicates a total population of nearly 4 million persons in the U.S. and western territories.

African Americans make up 19 percent of the population, with 90 percent living in the South.

Native Americans were not counted.

1791 CE

Cherokee Treaty

A Treaty of Peace and; Friendship made and concluded between the President of the United States of America, on the Part and Behalf of the said States, and the undersigned Chiefs and Warriors, of the Cherokee Nation of Indians, on the part aide Behalf of the said Nation.

The parties being desirous of establishing permanent peace and friendship between the United States and the said Cherokee Nation, and the citizens and members thereof, and to remove the causes of war, by ascertaining their limits and making other necessary, just and friendly arrangements: The President of the United States, by William Blount, Governor of the territory of the United States of America, south of the river Ohio, and Superintendant of Indian affairs for the southern district, who is vested with full powers for these purposes, by and with-the advice and consent of the Senate of the United States. And the Cherokee Nation, by the undersigned Chiefs and Warriors representing the said nation, have agreed to the following articles, namely:

ARTICLE I.

There shall be perpetual peace and friendship between all the citizens of the United States of America, and all the individuals composing the whole Cherokee nation of Indians.

ARTICLE II.

The undersigned Chiefs and Warriors, for themselves and all parts of the Cherokee nation do acknowledge themselves and the said Cherokee nation, to be under the protection of the said United States of America, and of no other sovereign whosoever; and they also stipulate that the said Cherokee nation will not hold any treaty with any foreign power, individual state, or with individuals of any state.

ARTICLE III.

The Cherokee nation shall deliver to the Governor of the territory of the United States of America, south of the river Ohio, on or before the first day of April next, at this place, all persons who are now prisoners, captured by them from any part of the United States: And the United States shall on or before the same day, and at the same place, restore to the Cherokees, all the prisoners now in captivity, which the citizens of the United States have captured from them.

ARTICLE IV.

The boundary between the citizens of the United States and the Cherokee nation, is and shall be as follows: Beginning at the top of the Currahee mountain, where the Creek line passes it; thence a direct line to Tugelo river; thence northeast to the Occunna mountain, and over the same along the South-Carolina Indian boundary to the North-Carolina boundary; thence north to a point from which a line is to be extended to the river Clinch, that shall pass the Holston at the ridge which divides the waters running into Little River from those running into the Tennessee; thence up the river Clinch to Campbell's line, and along the same to the top of Cumberland mountain; thence a direct line to the Cumberland river where the Kentucky road crosses it; thence down the Cumberland river to a point from which a south west line will strike the ridge which divides the waters of Cumberland from those of Duck river, forty miles above Nashville; thence down the said ridge to a point from whence a south west line will strike the mouth of Duck river.

And in order to preclude forever all disputes relative to the said boundary, the same shall be ascertained, and marked plainly by three persons appointed on the part of the United States, and three Cherokees on the part of their nation.

And in order to extinguish forever all claims of the Cherokee nation, or any part thereof, to any of the land lying to the right of the line above described. beginning as aforesaid at the Currahee mountain, it is hereby agreed, that in addition to the consideration heretofore made for the said land, the United States will cause certain valuable goods, to be immediately delivered to the undersigned Chiefs and Warriors, for the use of their nation; and the said United States will also cause the sum of one thousand dollars to be paid annually to the said Cherokee nation. And the undersigned Chiefs and Warriors, do hereby for themselves and the whole Cherokee nation, their heirs and descendants, for the considerations above-mentioned, release, quit-claim, relinquish and cede, all the land to the right of the line described, and beginning as aforesaid.

ARTICLE V.

It is stipulated and agreed, that the citizens and inhabitants of the United States, shall have a free and unmolested use of a road from Washington district to Mero district, and of the navigation of the Tennessee river.

ARTICLE VI.

It is agreed on the part of the Cherokees, that the United States shall have the sole and exclusive right of regulating their trade.

ARTICLE VII.

The United States solemnly guarantee to the Cherokee nation, all their lands not hereby ceded.

ARTICLE VIII.

If any citizen of the United States, or other person not being an Indian, shall settle on any of the Cherokees' lands, such person shall forfeit the protection of the United States, and the Cherokees may punish him or not, as they please.

ARTICLE IX.

No citizen or inhabitant of the United States, shall attempt to hunt or destroy the game on the lands of the Cherokees; nor shall any citizen or inhabitant go into the Cherokee country, without a passport first obtained from the Governor of some one of the United States, or territorial districts, or such other person as the President of the United States may from time to time authorize to grant the same.

ARTICLE X.

If any Cherokee Indian or Indians, or person residing among them, or who shall take refuge in their nation, shall steal a horse from, or commit a robbery or murder, or other capital crime, on any citizens or inhabitants of the United States, the Cherokee nation shall be bound to deliver him or them up, to be punished according to the laws of the United States.

ARTICLE XI.

If any citizen or inhabitant of the United States, or of either of the territorial districts of the United States, shall go into any town, settlement or territory belonging to the Cherokees, and shall there commit any crime upon, or trespass against the person or property of any peaceable and friendly Indian or Indians, which if committed within the jurisdiction of any state, or within the jurisdiction of either of the said districts, against a citizen or white inhabitant thereof, would be punishable by the laws of such state or district, such offender or offenders, shall be subject to the same punishment, and shall be proceeded against in the same manner as if the of fence had been committed within the jurisdiction of the state or district to which he or they may belong against a citizen or white inhabitant thereof.

ARTICLE XII.

In case of violence on the persons or property of the individuals of either party, neither retaliation or reprisal shall be committed by the other, until satisfaction shall have been demanded of the party of which the aggressor is and shall have been refused.

ARTICLE XIII.

The Cherokees shall give notice to the citizens of the United States, of any designs which they may know, or suspect to be formed in any neighboring tribe, or by any person whatever, against the peace and interest of the United States.

ARTICLE XIV.

That the Cherokee nation may be led to a greater degree of civilization, and to become herdsmen and cultivators, instead of remaining in a state of hunters, the United States will from time to time furnish gratuitously the said nation with useful implements of husbandry, and further to assist the said nation in so desirable a pursuit, and at the same time to establish a certain mode of communication, the United States will send such, and so many persons to reside in said nation as they may judge proper, not exceeding four in number, who shall qualify themselves to act as interpreters. These persons shall have lands assigned by the Cherokees for cultivation for themselves and their successors in office; but they shall be precluded exercising any kind of traffic.

ARTICLE XV.

All animosities for past grievances shall henceforth cease, and the contracting parties will carry the foregoing treaty into full execution with all good faith and sincerity.

ARTICLE XVI.

This treaty shall take effect and be obligatory on the contracting parties as soon as the same shall have been ratified by the President of the United States, with the advice and consent of the Senate of the United States. In witness of all and every thing herein determined between the United States of America and the whole Cherokee nation, the parties have hereunto set their hands and seals, at the treaty ground on the bank of the Holston, near the mouth of the French Broad, within the United States, this second day of July, in the year of our Lord one thousand seven hundred and ninety-one.

William Blount, governor in and over the territory of the United States of America south of the river Ohio, and superintendent of Indian Affairs for the southern district,

Chuleoah, or the Boots, his x mark,

Squollecuttah, or Hanging Maw, his x mark,

Oecunna,or the Badger,his x mark,

Enoleh, or Black Fox, his x mark,

Nontuaka, or the Northward, his x mark,

Tekakiska, his x mark

Chutloh, or King Fisher, his x mark,

Tuckaseh,orTerrapin,his x mark,

Kateh, his x mark

Kunnochatutloh, or the Crane, his x mark

Canquillehanah, or the Thigh, his x mark,

Chesquotteleneh, or Yellow Bird, his x mark,

Chickasawtehe, or Chickasaw Killer, his x mark,

Tuskegatehe, Tuskega Killer, his x mark,

Kulsatehe, his x mark,

Tinkshalene, his x mark

Sawntteh, or Slave Catcher, his x mark,

Auknah, his x mark

Oosenaleh, his x mark

Kenotetah, or Rising Fawn, his x mark,

Kanetetoka, or Standing Turkey, his x mark.

Yonewatleh, or Bear at Home, his x mark,

Long Will, his x mark

Kunoskeskie, or John Watts, his x mark,

Nenetooyah, or Bloody Fellow, his x mark,

Chuquilatague, or Double Head his x mark,

Koolaquah, or Big Acorn, his x mark

Too wayelloh, or Bold Hunter, his x mark

Jahleoonoyehka, or Middle Striker, his x mark,

Kinnesah, or Cabin, his x mark,

Tullotehe, or Two Killer, his x mark

Kaalouske, or Stopt Still, his x mark

Kulsatche, his x mark,

Auquotague, the Little Turkey's Son, his x mark,

Talohteske, or Upsetter, his x mark,

Cheakoneske, or Otter Lifter, his x mark

Keshukaune, or She Reigns, his x mark,

Toonaunailoh, his x mark,

Teesteke, or Common Disturber his x mark,

Robin McClemore

Skyuka

John Thompson, Interpreter.

James Cery, Interpreter.

Done in presence of-

Dan'l Smith, Secretary Territory United States south of the river Ohio

Thomas Kennedy, of Kentucky.
Jas. Robertson, of Mero District
Claiborne Watkins, of Virginia.
Jno. McWhitney, of Georgia.
Fauche, of Georgia.
Titus Ogden, North Carolina.
Jno. Chisolm, Washington District.
Robert King.
Thomas Gegg.

Additional Article To the Treaty made between the United States and the Cherokees on the second day of July, one thousand seven hundred and ninety-one.

IT is hereby mutually agreed between Henry Knox, Secretary of War, duly authorized thereto in behalf of the United States, on the one part, and the undersigned chiefs and warriors, in behalf of them selves and the

Cherokee nation, on the other part, that the following article shall be added to and considered as part of the treaty made between the United States and the said Cherokee nation on the second day of July, one thousand seven hundred and ninety-one; to wit:

The sum to be paid annually by the United States to the Cherokee nation of Indians, in consideration of the relinquishment of land, as stated in the treaty made with them on the second day of July, one thousand seven hundred and ninety-one, shall be one thousand five hundred dollars instead of one thousand dollars, mentioned in the said treaty.

In testimony whereof, the said Henry Knox, Secretary of War, and the said chiefs and warriors of the Cherokee nation, have hereunto set their hands and seals, in the city of Philadelphia, this seventeenth day of February, in the year of our Lord, one thousand seven hundred and ninety-two.

H. Knox, Secretary of War,
Iskagua, or Clear Sky, his x mark (formerly Nenetooyah,

or Bloody Fellow),

Nontuaka, or the Northward, his x mark,

Chutloh, or King Fisher, his x mark,

Katigoslah, or the Prince, his x mark,

Teesteke, or Common Disturber, his x mark,

Suaka, or George Miller, his x mark,

In presence of-

Thomas Grooter.

Jno. Stagg, Jr.

Leonard D. Shaw

James Cery, sworn intrepreter to the Cherokee Nation.

1791 CE

Fort Hamilton (Hamilton, Ohio – Butler county) was completed Sept. 30, 1791, and occupied by the U. S. Army commanded by Gen. Arthur St. Clair.

The supply base was the first in a chain of outposts north of Cincinnati (Fort Washington) in the Northwest Territory.

The log structure also supplied the victorious army of Gen. Anthony Wayne, 1792-1795.

Completion of the fort is considered Hamilton's founding date.

1791 CE

Native Americans inhabited and used much of the land in the Ohio valley as hunting grounds. As American settlers pushed west, conflicts resulted and attempts at peaceful settlement failed.

Under political pressure, President George Washington resolved to subdue Indian resistance to American expansion in the Ohio country and appointed General Arthur St. Clair to lead the expedition.

St. Clair's troops camped on the Wabash River (just east of the Ohio-Indiana state line) after an exhausting two month trek.

Major General Arthur St. Clair Commander-In-Chief of the American Army with fourteen or fifteen hundred regulars and volunteers from Virginia, Maryland, Pennsylvania, Kentucky, and that section of the North West Territory which comprises the states of Ohio and Indiana, marched from Fort Washington, now Cincinnati, in September of 1791 to subdue the Indians, who, under British influence, had committed many hostilities.

St. Clair was looking for the forces of Michikinikwa (Chief Little Turtle), who had recently defeated Gen. Josiah Harmar's army.

After a long weary march they reached the head waters of the Wabash River, where before daybreak on the following morning November 4th 1791, they were surprised and attacked by two thousand Indians of the Miami, Delaware, Pawnee, Shawnee, Wyandot, Seneca, and Ottawa tribes, under the command of the famous chiefs, Little Turtle, Blue Jacket, and Joseph Brandt, aided by the renegades Simon Girty, William Wells, and Blackstaffe.

The soldiers fought bravely in this unequal contest, but were forced to retreat leaving more than nine hundred men dead and wounded on the battle field.

Two hundred and fifty women accompanying the expedition were either killed or taken prisoners.

Gen. Arthur St. Clair, the territorial Governor, made the second attempt with a badly trained army. He marched north from Fort Washington (Cincinnati) and reached this place on the evening of Nov. 3, 1791.

The following morning, the army found itself surrounded by an Indian force commanded by Chief Little Turtle.

After a furious battle, St. Clair's troops broke through the enemy encirclement and retreated southward.

Here on this field they left approximately 900 dead and wounded, in what is relatively, the most disastrous defeat ever to befall an American Army.

The ill-prepared soldiers were no match for the forces of Miami, Shawnee, and Delaware Indians who attacked them at dawn of November 4, 1791.

By the day's end, warriors led by Little Turtle and Blue Jacket had killed or wounded nearly three-quarters of the American force - the worst-ever defeat of the U.S. Army by Native Americans in a single battle, General Arthur St. Clair, governor of Northwest Territory, was badly defeated by a large Indian army near Fort Wayne.

1793 CE

Gen. Mad Anthony Wayne led a third expedition against the Indians.

On this site where St. Clair met defeat, he built a post significantly named Fort Recovery, Dec. 23-26, 1793. Here was won the Battle of Fort Recovery, the most significant victory of the Indian Wars.

1794 CE

Early in the morning of June 30, 1794, a force of nearly 2,000 Indians under Chief Little Turtle, together with Canadian militiamen and British Officers, attacked a supply convoy near Fort Recovery.

This detachment retreated within the stockade after losing its commander, Maj. William McMahon.

The battle continued into the following day.

Then the Indians retreated, beaten and divided, never again to gather in such force to challenge Wayne.

1794 CE June

Cherokee Treaty

WHEREAS the treaty made and concluded on Holston river, on the second day of July, one thousand seven hundred and ninety-one, between the United States of America and the Cherokee nation of Indians, has not been fully carried into execution by reason of some misunderstandings which have arisen:

ARTICLE I.

And whereas the undersigned Henry Knox, Secretary for the department of War, being authorized thereto by the President of the United States, in behalf of the said United States, and the undersigned Chiefs and Warriors, in their own names, and in behalf of the whole Cherokee nation, are desirous of re-establishing peace and friendship between the said parties in a permanent manner, Do hereby declare, that the said treaty of Holston is, to all intents and purposes, in full force and binding upon the said parties, as well in respect to the boundaries therein mentioned as in all other respects whatever.

ARTICLE II.

It is hereby stipulated that the boundaries mentioned in the fourth article of the said treaty, shall be actually ascertained and marked in the manner prescribed by the said article, whenever the Cherokee nation shall have ninety days notice of the time and place at which the commissioners of the United States intend to commence their operation.

ARTICLE III.

The United States, to evince their justice by amply compensating the said Cherokee nation of Indians for all relinquishments of land made either by the treaty of Hopewell upon the Keowee river, concluded on the twenty-eighth of November one thousand seven hundred and eighty-five, or the aforesaid treaty made upon Holston river, on the second of July, one thousand seven hundred and ninety-one, do hereby stipulate, in lieu of all former slims to be paid annually to furnish the Cherokee Indians with goods suitable for their use, to the amount of five thousand dollars yearly.

ARTICLE IV.

And the said Cherokee nation, in order to evince the sincerity of their intentions in future, to prevent the practice of stealing horses, attended with the most pernicious consequences to the lives and peace of both parties, do hereby agree, that for every horse which shall be stolen from the white inhabitants by any Cherokee Indians, and not returned within three months, that the sum of fifty dollars shall be deducted from the said annuity of five thousand dollars.

ARTICLE V.

The articles now stipulated will be considered as permanent additions to the treaty of Holston, as soon as they shall have been ratified by the President of the United States and the Senate of the United States.

In witness of all and every thing herein determined between the United States of America and the whole Cherokee nation, the parties have hereunto set their hands and seals in the city of Philadelphia, within the United States, this twenty-sixth day of June, in the year of our Lord one thousand seven hundred and ninety four.

H. Knox, Secretary of War

Tekakisskee, or Taken out of the Water, his x mark

Nontuaka, or the North arc, his x mark,

Cinasaw, or the Cabin, his x mark,

Skyuka his x mark,

Chuquiiatague, or Double Head, his x mark

John MeCleemore, his x mark

Walaliue, or the Humming Bird,

Chuleowee, his x mark,

Ustanaqua, his X mark

Kullusathee, his x mark,

Siteaha, his x mark,

Keenaguna, or the Lying Fawn, his x mark,

Chatakaelesa, or the Fowl Carrier,

Done in presence of-

John Thompson,

William Wofford, of the State of Georgia.

Arthur Coodey, Interpreters,

W: McCaleb, of South Carolina.

Cantwell Jones, of Delaware.

Samuel Lewis, of Philadelphia.

1794 CE Aug 20

American General "Mad Anthony" Wayne defeated the Ohio Indians at the Battle of Fallen Timbers in the Northwest territory, ending Indian resistance in the area.

1794 CE

The Treaty of Canandaigua was signed at Canandaigua, New York, by fifty sachems and war chiefs representing the Grand Council of the Six Nations of the Iroquois (Haudenosaunee) Confederacy (including the Cayuga, Mohawk, Oneida, Onondaga, Seneca and Tuscarora tribes), and by Timothy Pickering, official agent of President George Washington.

The Canandaigua Treaty, a Treaty Between the United States of America and the Tribes of Indians Called the Six Nations, was signed.

A Treaty between the United States of America, and the Tribes of Indians called the Six Nations.

The President of the United States having determined to hold a conference with the Six Nations of Indians, for the purpose of removing from their minds all causes of complaint, and establishing a firm and permanent friendship with them; and Timothy Pickering being appointed sole agent for that purpose; and the agent having met and conferred with the Sachems, Chiefs and Warriors of the Six Nations, in a general council: Now, in order to accomplish the good design of this conference, the parties have agreed on the following articles; which, when ratified by the President, with the advice and consent of the Senate of the United States, shall be binding on them and the Six Nations.

ARTICLE I.

Peace and friendship are hereby firmly established, and shall be perpetual, between the United States and the Six Nations.

ARTICLE II.

The United States acknowledge the lands reserved to

the Oneida, Onondaga and Cayuga Nations, in their respective treaties with the state of New-York, and called their reservations, to be their property; and the United States will never claim the same nor disturb them or either of the Six Nations, nor their Indian friends residing thereon and united with them in the free use and enjoyment thereof: but the said reservations shall remain theirs, until they choose to sell the same to the people of the United States, who have the right to purchase.

ARTICLE III.

The land of the Seneka nation is bounded as follows: Beginning on Lake Ontario, at the north-west corner of the land they sold to

Oliver Phelps, the line runs westerly along the lake, as far as O-yong-wong-yeh Creek, at Johnson's Landing-place, about four miles eastward d from the fort of Niagara; then southerly up that creek to its main fork, then straight to the main fork of Stedman's creek, which empties into the river Niagara, above fort Schlosser, and then onward, from that fork, continuing the same straight course, to that river; (this line, from the mouth of O-yong-wong-yeh Creek to the river Niagara, above fort Schlosser, being the eastern boundary of a strip of land, extending from the same line to Niagara river, which the Seneka nation ceded to the King of Great-Britain, at a treaty held about thirty years ago, with Sir William Johnson;) then the line runs along the river Niagara to Lake Erie; then along Lake Erie to the north-east corner of a triangular piece of land which the United States conveyed to the state of Pennsylvania, as by the President's patent, dated the third day of March, 1792; then due south to the northern boundary of that state; then due east to the south-west corner of the land sold by the Seneka nation to Oliver Phelps; and then north and northerly, along Phelps's line, to the place of beginning on Lake Ontario. Now, the United States acknowledge all the land within the aforementioned boundaries, to be the property of the Seneka nation; and the United States will never claim the same, nor disturb the Seneka nation, nor any of the Six Nations, or of their Indian friends residing thereon and united with them, in the free use and enjoyment thereof: but it shall remain theirs, until they choose to sell tie same to the people of the United States, who have the right to purchase.

ARTICLE IV.

The United States having thus described and acknowledged what lands belong to the Oneidas, Onondagas, Cayugas and Senekas, and engaged never to claim the same, nor to disturb them, or any of the Six Nations, or their Indian friends residing thereon and united with them, in the free use and- enjoyment thereof: Now, the Six Nations, and each of them, hereby engage that they will never claim any other lands within the boundaries of the United States; nor ever disturb the people of the United States in the free use and enjoyment thereof.

ARTICLE V.

The Seneka nation, all others of the Six Nations concurring, cede to the United States the right of making a wagon road from Fort Schlosser to Lake Erie, as far south as Buffaloe Creek; and the people of the United States shall have the free and undisturbed use of this road, for the purposes of travelling and transportation. And the Six Nations, and each of them, will forever allow to the people of the United States, a free passage through their lands, and the free use of the harbors and rivers adjoining and within their respective tracts of land, for the passing and securing of vessels and boats, and liberty to land their cargoes where necessary for their safety.

ARTICLE VI.

In consideration of the peace and friendship hereby established, and of the engagements entered into by the Six Nations; and because the United States desire, with humanity and kindness, to contribute to their comfortable support; and to render the peace and friendship hereby established, strong and perpetual; the United States now deliver to the Six Nations, and the Indians of the other nations residing among and united with them, a quantity of goods of the value of ten thousand dollars. And for the same considerations, and with a view to promote the future welfare of the Six Nations, and of their Indian friends aforesaid, the United States will add the sum of three thousand dollars to the one thousand five hundred dollars, heretofore allowed them by an article ratified by the President, on the twenty-third day of April, 1792;(1) making in the whole, four thousand five hundred dollars; which shall be expended yearly forever, in purchasing clothing, domestic animals, implements of husbandry and other utensils suited to their circumstances, and in compensating useful artificers, who shall reside with or near them, and be employed for their benefit. The immediate application of the whole annual allowance now stipulated, to be made by the superintendent appointed by the President for the affairs of the Six Nations, and their Indian friends aforesaid.

ARTICLE VII.

Lest the firm peace and friendship now established should be interrupted by the misconduct of individuals, the United States and Six Nations agree, that for injuries done by individuals on either side, no private revenge or retaliation shall take place; but, instead thereof, complaint shall be made by the party injured to the other: BY the Six Nations or any of them, to the President of the United States, or the Superintendent by him appointed: and by the Superintendent, or other person appointed by the President, to the principal chiefs of the Six Nations, or of the nation to which the offender belongs: and such prudent measures shall then be pursued as shall be necessary to preserve our peace and friendship unbroken; until the legislature (or great council) of the United States shall make other equitable provision for the purpose.

NOTE. It is clearly understood by the parties to this treaty, that the annuity stipulated in the sixth article, is to be applied to the benefit of such of the Six Nations and of their Indian friends united with them as aforesaid, as do or shall reside within the boundaries of the United States: For the United States do not interfere with nations, tribes or families, of Indians elsewhere resident.

In witness whereof, the said Timothy Pickering, and the sachems and war chiefs of the said Six Nations, have hereto set their hands and seals.

Done at Konondaigua, in the State of New York, the eleventh day of November in the year one thousand seven hundred and ninety four.

Timothy Pickering,

Onoyeahnee, his x mark,

Konneatorteeooh, his x mark, or Handsome Lake,

Tokenhyonhau, his x mark, alias Captain Key

Oneshauee, his x mark

Hendrick Aupaurnut,

David Neesoonhuk his x mark,

Kanatsoyh, alias Nicholas Kusik,

Sohhonteoquent, his x mark

Ooduhtsait, his x mark,

Konoohqung, his x mark

Tossonggaulolus, his x mark,

John Skenendoa, his x mark

Oneatorleeooh, his x mark,

Kussanwatau, his x mark,

Eyootenyootanook, his x mark,

Kohnyeaugong, his x mark, alias Jake Stroud

Shaguiesa, his x mark

Teeroos, his x mark, alias Captain Prantup,

Sooshaoowau, his x mark,

Henry Young Brant, his x mark

Sonhyoowauna, his x mark, or Big Sky

Onsahhah, his x mark

Eotoshahenh, his x mark,

Kaukondanalya, his x mark,

Nondiyauka, his x mark,

Kossishtowau, his x mark

Oojaugenta, his x mark, or Fish Carrier

Toheonggo, his x mark,

Ootaguasso, his x mark,

Joonondauwaonch, his x mark,

Kiyanhaonh, his x mark,

Ootaujeaugenh, his x mark, or Broken Axe

Tauhoondos, his x mark, or Open the Way,

Twaukewasha, his x mark,

Sequidongquee, his x mark, alias Little Beard,

Kodjeote, his x mark or Half Town,

Kenjauarlgus, his x mark, or Stinking Fish,

185

Soonohquaukau, his x mark,

Twenniyana, his x mark,

Jishkaaga, his x mark, or Green Grasshopper, alias
Little Billy

Tuggehshotta, his x mark,

Tehongyagauna, his x mark,

Tehongyoownsh, his x mark,

E;onneyoowesot, his x mark

Tioohquottakauna, his x mark, or Woods on Fire

Taoundaudeesh, his x mark

Honayawns, his x mark, alias Farmer's Brother,

Soggocyawauthau, his x mark alias Red Jacket

Konyootiayoo, his x mark

Sanhtakaongyees, his x Mark, or Two Skies of a length,

Ounnashattakau, his x mark,

Kaungyanehquee, his x mark,

Sooayoowau, his x mark,

Kanjeagaonh, his x mark, or Heap of Dogs

Soonoohshoowau, his x mark

Thaoowaunias, his x mark,

Soonongjoowau, his x mark,

Kiantu hauka, his x mark, alias Cornplanter,

Iiaunehshonggoo, his x mark,

Witnesses:

Israel Chapin.
William Shepard, jr.
James Smedley.
John Wickham.
Augustus Porter.
James K. Garnsev.
William Ewing.
Israel Chapin, jr.
Horatio Jones,
Joseph Smith,
Jasper Parish,
Interpreters.
Henry Abeele.

(It appears that this treaty was never ratified by the Senate. See American State Papers, Indian Affairs, Not. 1, p. 232. Also, post 1927.)

Treaty With the Oneida, etc.,

A treaty between the United States and the Oneida, Tuscorora and Stockbridge Indians, dwelling in the Country of the Oneidas.

WHEREAS, in the late war between Great-Britain and the United States of America, a body of the Oneida and Tuscorora and the Stockbridge Indians, adhered faithfully to the United States, and assisted them with their warriors; and in consequence of this adherence and assistance, the Oneidas and Tuscororas, at an unfortunate period of the war, were driven from their homes, and their houses were burnt and their property destroyed: And as the United States in the time of their distress, acknowledged their obligations to these faithful friends, and promised to reward them: and the United States being now in a condition to fulfil the promises then made: the following articles are stipulated by the respective parties for that purpose; to be in force when ratified by the President and Senate.

ARTICLE I.

The United States will pay the sum of five thousand dollars, to be distributed among individuals of the Oneida and Tuscorora nations, as a compensation for their individual losses and services during the late war between Great-Britain and the United States. The only man of the Kaughnawaugas now remaining in the Oneida country, as well as some few very meritorious persons of the Stockbridge Indians, will be considered in the distribution.

ARTICLE II.

For the general accommodation of these Indian nations, residing in the country of the Oneidas, the United States will cause to be erected a complete grist-mill and saw-mill, in a situation to serve the present principal settlements of these nations. Or if such one convenient situation cannot be found, then the United States will cause to be erected two such grist-mills and saw-mills, in places where it is now known the proposed accommodation may be effected. Of this the United

States will judge.

ARTICLE III.

The United States will provide, during three years after the mills shall be completed, for the expense of employing one or two suitable persons to manage the mills, to keep them in repair, to instruct some young men of the three nations in the arts of the miller and sawyer, and to provide teams and utensils for carrying on the work of the mills.

ARTICLE IV.

The United States will pay one thousand dollars, to be applied in building a convenient church at Oneida, in the place of the one which was there burnt by the enemy, in the late war.

ARTICLE V.

In consideration of the above stipulations to be performed on the part of the United States, the Oneida,

Tuscorora and Stockbridge Indians afore-mentioned, now acknowledge themselves satisfied, and relinquish all other claims of compensation and rewards for their losses and services in the late war. Excepting only the unsatisfied claims of such men of the said nations as bore commissions under the United States, for any arrears which may be due to them as officers.

In witness whereof, the chiefs of those nations, residing in the country of the Oneidas, and Timothy Pickering, agent for the United States have hereto set their hands and seals, at Oneida, the second day of December, in the year one thousand seven hundred and ninety four.

Timothy Pickering,

Wolf Tribe:

Odotsaihte, his x mark,
Konnoquenyau, his x mark,
Head sachems of the Oneidas.
John Skenendo, eldest war chief, his x mark,
Bear Tribe:

191

Lodowik Kohsanwetau,his x mark,

Cornelius Kauhiktoton, his x mark,

Thos. Osauhataugaunlot, his x mark

War chiefs.

Turtle Tribe:

Shonohleyo, warchief, his x mark,

PeterKonnauterlook, sachelll, his x mark.

Daniel Teouneslees, son of Sken endo. war chief. his x

Clark

Tuscaroras:

Thaulondauwaugon, sachem, his x mark,

Kanatjogh, or Nicholas Cusiek, war chief, his x mark,

Witnesses to the signing and sealing of the agent of the United States, and of the chiefs of the Oneida and Tuscarora nations:

S. Kirkland,
 James Dean, Interpreter.

Witnesses to the signing and sealing of the four chiefs of the Stockbridge Indians, whose names are below:

Saml. Kirkland,
John Sergeant.

Stockbridge Indians

Hendrick Aupaumut,
Joseph Quonney,
John Konkapot,
Jacob Konkapot,

1795 CE

The Treaty of Greenville 1795

A treaty of peace between the United States of America, and the tribes of Indians called the Wyandots, Delawares, Shawanees, Ottawas, Chippewas,

Pattawatimas, Miamis, Eel Rivers, Weas, Kickapoos, Piankeshaws, and Kaskaskias.

To put an end to a destructive war, to settle all controversies, and to restore harmony and friendly intercourse between the said United States and Indian tribes, Anthony Wayne, major general commanding the army of the United States, and sole commissioner for the good purposes above mentioned, and the said tribes of Indians, by their sachems, chiefs, and warriors, met together at Greenville, the head quarters of the said army, have agreed on the following articles, which, when ratified by the President, with the advice and consent of the Senate of the United States, shall be binding on them and the said Indian tribes.

Art. 1:

Henceforth all hostilities shall cease; peace is hereby established, and shall be perpetual; and a friendly intercourse shall take place between the said United States and Indian tribes.

Art. 2:

All prisoners shall, on both sides, be restored. The
Indians, prisoners to the United States, shall be
immediately set at liberty. The people of the United
States, still remaining prisoners among the Indians,
shall be delivered up in ninety days from the date
hereof, to the general or commanding officer at
Greenville, fort Wayne, or fort Defiance; and ten chiefs
of the said tribes shall remain at Greenville as hostages,
until the delivery of the prisoners shall be effected.

Art. 3:

The general boundary line between the lands of the
United States and the lands of the said Indian tribes,
shall begin at the mouth of Cayahoga river, and run
thence up the same to the portage, between that and
the Tuscarawas branch of the Muskingum, thence down
that branch to the crossing place above fort Lawrence,
thence westerly to a fork of that branch of the Great
Miami river, running into the Ohio, at or near which

fork stood Loromie's store, and where commences the portage between the Miami of the Ohio, and St. Mary's river, which is a branch of the Miami which runs into lake Erie; thence a westerly course to fort Recovery, which stands on a branch of the Wabash; thence southwesterly in a direct line to the Ohio, so as to intersect that river opposite the mouth of Kentucke or Cuttawa river. And in consideration of the peace now established; of the goods formerly received from the United States; of those now to be delivered; and of the yearly delivery of goods now stipulated to be made hereafter; and to indemnify the United States for the injuries and expenses they have sustained during the war, the said Indian tribes do hereby cede and relinquish forever, all their claims to the lands lying eastwardly and southwardly of the general boundary line now described: and these lands, or any part of them, shall never hereafter be made a cause or pretence, on the part of the said tribes, or any of them, of war or injury to the United States, or any of the people thereof.

And for the same considerations, and as an evidence of the returning friendship of the said Indian tribes, of their confidence in the United States, and desire to provide for their accommodations, and for that convenient intercourse which will be beneficial to both parties, the said Indian tribes do also cede to the United States the following pieces of land, to wit:

One piece of land six miles square, at or near Loromie's store, before mentioned.

One piece two miles square, at the head of the navigable water or landing, on the St. Mary's river, near Girty's town.

One piece six miles square, at the head of the navigable water of the Auglaize river.

One piece six miles square, at the confluence of the Auglaize and Miami rivers, where fort Defiance now stands.

One piece six miles square, at or near the confluence of the rivers St. Mary's and St. Joseph's, where fort Wayne now stands, or near it.

One piece two miles square, on the Wabash river, at the end of the portage from the Miami of the lake, and about eight miles westward from fort Wayne.

One piece six miles square, at the Ouatanon, or Old Wea towns, on the Wabash river. 8) One piece twelve miles square, at the British fort on the Miami of the lake, at the foot of the rapids.

One piece six miles square, at the mouth of the said river, where it empties into the lake.

One piece six miles square, upon Sandusky lake, where a fort formerly stood. One piece two miles square, at the lower rapids of Sandusky river.

The post of Detroit, and all the land to the north, the west and the south of it, of which the Indian title has been extinguised by gifts or grants to the French or

English governments: and so much more land to be annexed to the district of Detroit, as shall be comprehended between the river Rosine, on the south, lake St. Clair on the north, and a line, the general course whereof shall be six miles distant from the west end of lake Erie and Detroit river.

The post of Michilimackinac, and all the land on the island on which that post stands, and the main land adjacent, of which the Indian title has been extinguished by gifts or grants to the Frewnch or English governments; and a piece of land on the main to the north of the island, to measure six miles, on lake Huron, or the strait between lakes Huron and Michigan, and to extend three miles back from the water of the lake or strait; and also, the Island De Bois Blane, being an extra and voluntary gift of the Chippewa nation.

One piece of land six miles square, at the mouth of Chikago river, emptying into the southwest end of lake Michigan, where a fort formerly stood.

One piece twelve miles square, at or near the mouth of

the Illinois river, emptying into the Mississippi.

One piece six miles square, at the old Piorias fort and village near the south end of the Illinois lake, on said Illinois river. And whenever the United States shall think proper to survey and mark the boundaries of the lands hereby ceded to them, they shall give timely notice thereof to the said tribes of Indians, that they may appoint some of their wise chiefs to attend and see that the lines are run according to the terms of this treaty.

And the said Indian tribes will allow to the people of the United States a free passage by land and by water, as one and the other shall be found convenient, through their country, along the chain of posts hereinbefore mentioned; that is to say, from the commencement of the portage aforesaid, at or near Loromie's store, thence along said portage to the St. Mary's, and down the same to fort Wayne, and then down the Miami, to lake Erie; again, from the commencement of the portage at or near Loromie's store along the portage from thence to the river Auglaize, and down the same to its junction with the Miami at fort Defiance; again, from the commencement of the portage aforesaid, to Sandusky river, and down the same to Sandusky bay and lake Erie, and from Sandusky to the post which shall be taken at or near the foot of the Rapids of the Miami of the lake; and from thence to Detroit. Again, from the mouth of Chikago, to the commencement of the portage, between that river and the Illinois, and down the Illinois river to the Mississippi; also, from fort Wayne, along the portage aforesaid, which leads to the Wabash, and then down the Wabash to the Ohio. And the said Indian tribes will also allow to the people of the United States, the free use of the harbors and mouths of rivers along the lakes adjoining the Indian lands, for sheltering vessels and boats, and liberty to land their cargoes where necessary for their safety.

Art. 4:

In consideration of the peace now established, and of the cessions and relinquishments of lands made in the preceding article by the said tribes of Indians, and to manifest the liberality of the United States, as the great means of rendering this peace strong and perpetual, the

United States relinquish their claims to all other Indian lands northward of the river Ohio, eastward of the Mississippi, and westward and southward of the Great Lakes and the waters, uniting them, according to the boundary line agreed on by the United States and the King of Great Britain, in the treaty of peace made between them in the year 1783. But from this relinquishment by the United States, the following tracts of land are explicitly excepted:

1st. The tract on one hundred and fifty thousand acres near the rapids of the river Ohio, which has been assigned to General Clark, for the use of himself and his warriors.

2nd. The post of St. Vincennes, on the River Wabash, and the lands adjacent, of which the Indian title has been extinguished.

3rd. The lands at all other places in possession of the French people and other white settlers among them, of which the Indian title has been extinguished as mentioned in the 3d article;

and 4th. The post of fort Massac towards the mouth of the Ohio. To which several parcels of land so excepted, the said tribes relinquish all the title and claim which they or any of them may have.

And for the same considerations and with the same views as above mentioned, the United States now deliver to the said Indian tribes a quantity of goods to the value of twenty thousand dollars, the receipt whereof they do hereby acknowledge; and henceforward every year, forever, the United States will deliver, at some convenient place northward of the river Ohio, like useful goods, suited to the circumstances of the Indians, of the value of nine thousand five hundred dollars; reckoning that value at the first cost of the goods in the city or place in the United States where they shall be procured. The tribes to which those goods are to be annually delivered, and the proportions in which they are to be delivered, are the following:

1st. To the Wyandots, the amount of one thousand dollars.

2nd. To the Delawares, the amount of one thousand dollars.

3rd. To the Shawanees, the amount of one thousand dollars.

4th. To the Miamis, the amount of one thousand dollars.

5th. To the Ottawas, the amount of one thousand dollars.

6th. To the Chippewas, the amount of one thousand dollars.

7th.To the Pattawatimas, the amount of one thousand dollars, and 8th.

To the Kickapoo, Wea, Eel River, Piankeshaw, and Kaskaskia tribes, the amount of five hundred dollars each.

Provided, that if either of the said tribes shall hereafter, at an annual delivery of their share of the goods aforesaid, desire that a part of their annuity should be furnished in domestic animals, implements of husbandry, and other utensils convenient for them, and in compensation to useful artificers who may reside with or near them, and be employed for their benefit, the same shall, at the subsequent annual deliveries, be furnished accordingly.

Art. 5:

To prevent any misunderstanding about the Indian lands relinquished by the United States in the fourth article, it is now explicitly declared, that the meaning of that relinquishment is this: the Indian tribes who have a right to those lands, are quietly to enjoy them, hunting, planting, and dwelling thereon, so long as they please, without any molestation from the United States; but when those tribes, or any of them, shall be disposed to sell their lands, or any part of them, they are to be sold only to the United States; and until such sale, the United States will protect all the said Indian tribes in the quiet enjoyment of their lands against all citizens of the United States, and against all other white persons who intrude upon the same. And the said Indian tribes again acknowledge themselves to be under the protection of the said United States, and no other power whatever.

Art. 6:

If any citizen of the United States, or any other white person or persons, shall presume to settle upon the lands now relinquished by the United States, such citizen or other person shall be out of the protection of the United States; and the Indian tribe, on whose land the settlement shall be made, may drive off the settler, or punish him in such manner as they shall think fit; and because such settlements, made without the consent of the United States, will be injurious to them as well as to the Indians, the United States shall be at liberty to break them up, and remove and punish the settlers as they shall think proper, and so effect that protection of the Indian lands herein before stipulated.

Art. 7:

The said tribes of Indians, parties to this treaty, shall be at liberty to hunt within the territory and lands which they have now ceded to the United States, without hindrance or molestation, so long as they demean themselves peaceably, and offer no injury to the people of the United States.

Art. 8:

Trade shall be opened with the said Indian tribes; and they do hereby respectively engage to afford protection to such persons, with their property, as shall be duly licensed to reside among them for the purpose of trade; and to their agents and servants; but no person shall be permitted to reside among them for the purpose of trade; and to their agents and servants; but no person shall be permitted to reside at any of their towns or hunting camps, as a trader, who is not furnished with a license for that purpose, under the hand and seal of the superintendent of the department northwest of the Ohio, or such other person as the President of the United States shall authorize to grant such licenses; to the end, that the said Indians may not be imposed on in their trade.* And if any licensed trader shall abuse his privilege by unfair dealing, upon complaint and proof thereof, his license shall be taken from him, and he shall be further punished according to the laws of the United States. And if any person shall intrude himself as a trader, without such license, the said Indians shall take and bring him before the superintendent, or his deputy, to be dealt with according to law. And to prevent impositions by forged licenses, the said Indians shall, at lease once a year, give information to the superintendent, or his deputies, on the names of the traders residing among them.

Art. 9:

Lest the firm peace and friendship now established,

should be interrupted by the misconduct of individuals, the United States, and the said Indian tribes agree, that for injuries done by individuals on either side, no private revenge or retaliation shall take place; but instead thereof, complaint shall be made by the party injured, to the other: by the said Indian tribes or any of them, to the President of the United States, or the superintendent by him appointed; and by the superintendent or other person appointed by the President, to the principal chiefs of the said Indian tribes, or of the tribe to which the offender belongs; and such prudent measures shall then be taken as shall be necessary to preserve the said peace and friendship unbroken, until the legislature (or great council) of the United States, shall make other equitable provision in the case, to the satisfaction of both parties. Should any Indian tribes meditate a war against the United States, or either of them, and the same shall come to the knowledge of the before mentioned tribes, or either of them, they do hereby engage to give immediate notice thereof to the general, or officer commanding the troops of the United States, at the nearest post.

And should any tribe, with hostile intentions against the United States, or either of them, attempt to pass through their country, they will endeavor to prevent the same, and in like manner give information of such attempt, to the general, or officer commanding, as soon as possible, that all causes of mistrust and suspicion may be avoided between them and the United States. In like manner, the United States shall give notice to the said Indian tribes of any harm that may be meditated against them, or either of them, that shall come to their knowledge; and do all in their power to hinder and prevent the same, that the friendship between them may be uninterrupted.

Art. 10:

All other treaties heretofore made between the United States, and the said Indian tribes, or any of them, since the treaty of 1783, between the United States and Great Britain, that come within the purview of this treaty, shall henceforth cease and become void.

In testimony whereof, the said Anthony Wayne, and the sachems and war chiefs of the before mentioned nations and tribes of Indians, have hereunto set their hands and affixed their seals. Done at Greenville, in the territory of the United States northwest of the river Ohio, on the third day of August, one thousand seven hundred and ninety five.

WYANDOTS.

Tarhe, or Crane, his x mark
J. Williams, jun. his x mark,
Teyyaghtaw, his x mark,
Haroenyou, or half king's son, his x mark,
Tehaawtorens, his x mark,
Awmeyeeray, his x mark,
Stayetah, his x mark
Shateyyaronyah, or Leather Lips, his x mark,
Daughshuttayah, his x mark
Shaawrunthe, his x mark

DELAWARES.

Tetabokshke, or Grand Glaize King, his x mark,

Lemantanquis, or Black King, his x mark,

Wabatthoe, his x mark,

Maghpiway, or Red Feather, his x mark,

Kikthawenund, or Anderson, his x mark,

Bukongehelas, his x mark,

Peekeelund, his x mark,

Wellebawkeelund, his x mark,

Peekeetelemund, or Thomas Adams, his x mark,

Kishkopekund, or Captain Buffalo, his x mark,

Amenahehan, or Captain Crow, his x mark,

Queshawksey, or George Washington, his x mark,

Weywinquis, or Billy Siscomb, his x mark,

Moses, his x mark,

SHAWANEES.

Misquacoonacaw, or Red Pole, his x mark,

Cutthewekasaw, or Black Hoof, his x mark,

Kaysewaesekah, his x mark,

Weythapamattha, his x mark,

Nianysmeka, his x mark,

Waytheah, or Long Shanks, his x mark,

Weyapiersenwaw, or Blue Jacket, his x mark,

Nequetaughaw, his x mark,

Hahgoosekaw, or Captain Reed, his x mark,

OTTAWAS.

Augooshaway, his x mark,

Keenoshameek, his x mark,

La Malice, his x mark,

Machiwetah, his x mark,

Thowonawa, his x mark,

Secaw, his x mark,

CHIPPEWAS.

Mashipinashiwish, or Bad Bird, his x mark,

Nahshogashe, (from Lake Superior), his x mark,

Kathawasung, his x mark,

Masass, his x mark,

Nemekass, or Little Thunder, his x mark,

Peshawkay, or Young Ox, his x mark,

Nanguey, his x mark,

Meenedohgeesogh, his x mark,

Peewanshemenogh, his x mark,

Weymegwas, his x mark,

Gobmaatick, his x mark,

OTTAWA.

Chegonickska, an Ottawa from Sandusky, his x mark,

PATTAWATIMAS OF THE RIVER ST. JOSEPH.

Thupenebu, his x mark,

Nawac, for himself and brother Etsimethe, his x mark,

Nenanseka, his x mark,

Keesass, or Run, his x mark,

Kabamasaw, for himself and brother Chisaugan, his x mark,

Sugganunk, his x mark,

Wapmeme, or White Pigeon, his x mark,

Wacheness, for himself and brother Pedagoshok, his x mark, Wabshicawnaw, his x mark, La Chasse, his x mark, Meshegethenogh, for himself and brother,

Wawasek, his x mark,

Hingoswash, his x mark,

Anewasaw, his x mark, Nawbudgh, his x mark,

Missenogomaw, his x mark, L.S. Waweegshe, his x mark,

Thawme, or Le Blanc, his x mark,

Geeque, for himself and brother Shewinse, his x mark,

PATTAWATIMAS OF HURON.

Okia, his x mark,

Chamung, his x mark,

Segagewan, his x mark,

Nanawme, for himself and brother A. Gin, his x mark,

Marchand, his x mark, Wenameac, his x mark,

MIAMIS.

Nagohquangogh, or Le Gris, his x mark,

Meshekunnoghquoh, or Little Turtle, his x mark,

MIAMIS AND EEL RIVERS.

Peejeewa, or Richard Ville, his x mark,

Cochkepoghtogh, his x mark,

EEL RIVER TRIBE.

Shamekunnesa, or Soldier, his x mark, L.S.

MIAMIS.

Wapamangwa, or the White Loon, his x mark,

WEAS, FOR THEMSELVES AND THE PIANKESHAWS.

Amacunsa, or Little Beaver, his x mark,
Acoolatha, or Little Fox, his x mark,
Francis, his x mark,

KICKAPOOS AND KASKASKIAS.

Keeawhah, his x mark,
Nemighka, or Josey Renard, his x mark,
Paikeekanogh, his x mark,

DELAWARES OF SANDUSKY.

Hawkinpumiska, his x mark,
Peyamawksey, his x mark,
Reyntueco, (of the Six Nations, living at Sandusky), his
x mark,

H. De Butts, first A.D.C. and Sec'ry to Major Gen.
Wayne,
Wm. H. Harrison, Aid de Camp to Major Gen. Wayne,
T. Lewis, Aid de Camp to Major Gen. Wayne,
James O'Hara, Quartermaster Gen'l.
John Mills, Major of Infantry, and Adj. Gen'l. Caleb
Swan,
P.M.T.U.S. Gen. Demter, Lieut. Artillery,
Vigo,
P. Frs. La Fontaine, Ast. Lasselle,

Sworn interpreters.
H. Lasselle, Wm. Wells,
Js. Beau Bien, Jacques Lasselle,
David Jones, Chaplain U.S.S. M. Morins,
Lewis Beaufait,

Bt. Sans Crainte,

R. Lachambre,

Christopher Miller,

Jas. Pepen,

Robert Wilson,

Baties Coutien,

Abraham Williams, his x mark

P. Navarre.

Isaac Zane, his x mark

(The United States continued to gain title to Native American land after the Treaty of Greenville, at a rate that created alarm in Indian communities.

In 1800, William Henry Harrison became governor of the Indiana Territory and, under the direction of President Thomas Jefferson, pursued an aggressive policy of obtaining titles to Indian lands. Two Shawnee brothers, Tecumseh and Tenskwatawa, organized another pan-tribal resistance to American expansion.

While Tecumseh was in the south attempting to recruit allies among the Creeks, Cherokees, and Choctaws, Harrison marched against the Indian confederacy, defeating Tenskwatawa and his followers at the Battle of Tippecanoe in 1811.

The Americans hoped that the victory would end the militant resistance, but Tecumseh instead chose to openly ally with the British, who were soon at war with the Americans in the War of 1812.

Like the Revolutionary War, the War of 1812 was also a massive war on the western front.

Encouraged by Tecumseh, the Creek War (1813–1814), which began as a civil war within the Creek (Muscogee) nation, became part of the larger struggle against American expansion.

Although the war with the British was a stalemate, the United States was more successful on the western front.

Tecumseh was killed by Harrison's army at the Battle of

219

the Thames, ending the resistance in the Old Northwest.

As in the Revolution and the Northwest Indian War, after the War of 1812, the British abandoned their Indian allies to the Americans.

This proved to be a major turning point in the Indian Wars, marking the last time that Native Americans would turn to a foreign power for assistance against the United States.)

1795 CE

Fort St. Marys, aka: "Girty's Town" erected by General "Mad" Anthony Wayne on land and near Indian campsites to the south and west ceded by the Indians.

1797 CE

Treaty with the Mohawk

Relinquishment to New York, by the Mohawk nation of Indians, under the sanction of the United States of

America, of all claim to lands in that state.

AT a treaty held under the authority of the United States, with the Mohawk nation of Indians, residing in the province of Upper Canada, within the dominions of the king of Great Britain, present, the honorable Isaac Smith, commissioner appointed by the United States to hold this treaty; Abraham Ten Broeck, Egbert Benson, and Ezra L'Hommedieu, agents for the state of New York; captain Joseph Brandt, and captain John Deserontyon, two of the said Indians and deputies, to represent the said nation at this treaty.

The said agents having, in the presence, and with the approbation of the said commissioner, proposed to and adjusted with the said deputies, the compensation as hereinafter mentioned to be made to the said nation, for their claim, to be extinguished by this treaty, to all lands within the said state: it is thereupon finally agreed and done, between the said agents, and the said deputies, as follows, that is to say: the said agents do agree to pay to the said deputies, the sum of one thousand dollars, for the use of the said nation, to be by the said deputies paid over to, and distributed among, the persons and families of the said nation, according to their usages. The sum of five hundred dollars, for the expenses of the said deputies, during the time they have attended this treaty: and the sum of one hundred dollars, for their expenses in returning, and for conveying the said sum of one thousand dollars, to where the said nation resides. And the said agents do accordingly, for and in the name of the people of the state of New York, pay the said three several sums to the said deputies, in the presence of the said commissioner. And the said deputies do agree to cede and release, and these presents witness, that they accordingly do, for and in the name of the said nation, in consideration of the said compensation, cede and release to the people of the state of New York, forever, all the right or title of the said nation to lands within the said state: and the claim of the said nation to lands within the said state, is hereby wholly and finally extinguished.

In testimony whereof, the said commissioner, the said agents, and the said deputies, have hereunto, and to two other acts of the same tenor and date, one to remain with the United States, one to remain with the said State, and one delivered to the said deputies, to remain with the said nation, set their hands and seals, at the city of Albany, in the said State, the twenty-ninth day of March, in the year one thousand seven hundred and ninety-seven.

Isaac Smith,
Abm. Ten Broeck,
Egbt. Benson,
Ezra L'Hommedieu,
Jos. Brandt,
John Deserontyon,
Witnesses:
Robert Yates,
John Tayler,
Chas. Williamson,
Thomas Morris,
The mark of x John Abeel, alias the Cornplanter, a chief of the Senekas.

Agreement With The Seneca

Contract entered into, under the sanction of the United States of America, between Robert Morris and the Seneca nation of Indians.

This indenture, made the fifteenth day of September, in the year of our Lord one thousand seven hundred and ninety-seven, between the sachems, chiefs, and warriors of the Seneca nation of Indians, of the first part, and Robert Morris, of the city of Philadelphia, Esquire, of the second part:

Whereas the Commonwealth of Massachusetts have granted, bargained, and sold unto the said Robert Morris, his heirs and assigns forever, the pre-emptive right, and all other the right, title and interest which the said Commonwealth had to all the tract of land hereinafter particularly mentioned, being part of a tract of land lying within the State of New York, the right of pre-emption of the soil whereof, from the native Indians, was ceded and granted by the said State of New York, to

the said Commonwealth: and whereas, at a treaty held
under the authority of the United States, with the said
Seneca nation of Indians, at Genesee, in the county of
Ontario, and State of New York, on the day of the date of
these presents, and on sundry days immediately prior
thereto, by the Honorable Jeremiah Wadsworth,
Esquire, a commissioner appointed by the President of
the United States, to hold the same in pursuance of the
constitution, and of the act of the Congress of the
United States, in such case made and provided, it was
agreed, in the presence and with the approbation of the
said commissioner, by the sachems, chiefs and warriors
of the said nations of Indians, for themselves and in
behalf of their nation, to sell to the said Robert Morris,
and to his heirs and assigns forever, all their right to all
that tract of land above recited, and hereinafter
particularly specified, for the sum of one hundred
thousand dollars, to be by the said Robert Morris vested
in the stock of the bank of the United States, and held
in the name of the President of the United States, for the
use and behoof of the said nation of Indians, the said
agreement and sale being also made in the presence,
and with the approbation of the honorable William

Shepard, Esquire, the superintendent appointed for such purpose, in pursuance of a resolve of the General Court of the Commonwealth of Massachusetts, passed the eleventh day of March, in the year of our Lord one thosuand seven hundred and ninety-one; now this indenture witnesseth, that the said parties, of the first part, for and in consideration of the premises above recited, and for divers other good and valuable considerations them thereunto moving, have granted, bargained, sold, aliened, released, enfeoffed, and confirmed; and by these presents do grant, bargain, sell, alien, release, enfeoff, and confirm, unto the said party of the second part, his heirs and assigns forever, all that certain tract of land, except as is hereinafter excepted, lying within the county of Ontario and State of New York, being part of a tract of land, the right of pre-emption whereof was ceded by the state of New York to the Commonwealth of Massachusetts, by deed of cession executed at Hartford, on the sixteenth day of December, in the year of our Lord one thousand seven hundred and eighty-six, being all such part thereof as is not included in the Indian purchase made by Oliver Phelps and Nathaniel Gorham, and bounded as follows,

226

to wit: easterly, by the land confirmed to Oliver Phelps and Nathaniel Gorham by the legislature of the Commonwealth of Massachusetts, by and act passed the twenty-first day of November, in the year of our Lord one thousand seven hundred and eighty-eight; southerly, by the north boundary line of the State of Pennsylvania; westerly, partly by a tract of land, part of the land ceded by the State of Massachusetts to the United States, and by them sold to Pennsylvania, being a righ' angled triangle, whose hypothenuse is in or along the shore of Lake Erie; partly by Lake Erie, from the northern point of that triangle to the Southern bounds of a tract of land a mile in width, lying on and along the east side of the strait of Niagara, and partly by the said tract to lake Ontario; and on the north, by the boundary line between the United States and the King of Great Britain; excepting, nevertheless, and reserving always out of this grant and conveyance, all such pieces or parcels of the aforesaid tract, and such privileges thereunto belonging as are next hereinafter mentioned, which said pieces or parcels of land so excepted are, by the parties to these presents, clearly and fully understood to remain the property of the said parties of

227

the first part, in as full and ample manner as if these presents had not been executed; that is to say, excepting and reserving to them, the said parties of the first part, and their nation, one piece or parcel of the aforesaid tract, at Canawaugas, of two square miles, to be laid out in such manner as to include the village extending in breadth one mile along the river; one other piece or parcel at Big Tree, of two square miles, to be laid out in such manner as to include the village, extending in breadth along the river one mile; one other piece or parcel of two square miles at Little Beard's town, extending one mile along the river, to be laid off in such manner as to include the village; one other tract of two square miles at Squawky Hill, to be laid off as follows, to wit: one square mile to be laid off along the river, in such manner as to include the village, the other directly west thereof and contiguo's thereto; one other piece or parcel at Gardeau, beginning at the mouth of Steep Hill creek, thence due east until it strikes the old path, thence south until a due west line will intersect with certain steep rocks on the west side of Genesee river, then extending due west, due north and due east, until it strikes the first mentiones bound, enclosing as much land on the west side as on the east side of the river. One other piece or parcel at Kaounadeau extending in length eight miles along the river and two miles in breadth. One other piece or parcel at Cataraugos, beginning at the mouth of the Eighteen mile or Koghquaugu creek, thence a line or line to be drawn parallel to lake Erie, at the distance of one mile from there, to the mouth of Cataraugos creek, thence a line or lines extending 12 miles up the north side of said creek at the distance of one mile thereform, thence a direct line to the said creek, thence down the said creek to lake Erie, thence along the lake to the first mentioned creek, and thence to the place of beginning. Also one other piece at Cataraugos, beginning at the shore of lake Erie, on the south side of Cataraugos creek, at the distance of one mile from the mouth thereof, thence running one mile from the lake, thence on a line parallel thereto, to a point within one mile from the Connondauweyea creek, thence up the said creek one mile, on a line parallel thereto, thence on a direct line to the said creek, thence down the same to lake Erie, thence along the lake to the place of beginning. Also one other piece or parcel of forty-two square miles, at or near the Allegenny river. Also, two hundred square miles, to be laid off partly at the Buffalo and partly at the Tonnawanta creeks. Also, excepting and reserving to them, the said parties of the first part and their heirs, the privilege of fishing and hunting on the said tract of land hereby intended to be conveyed. And it is hereby understood by and between the parties to these presents, that all such pieces or parcels of land as are hereby reserved and are not particularly described as to the manner in which the same are to be laid off, shall be laid off in such manner as shall be determined by the sachems, chiefs, residing at or near the respective villages where such reservations are made, a particular note whereof to be indorsed on the back of this deed, and recorded therewith, together with all and singular the rights, privileges, hereditaments, and appurtenances thereunto belonging, or in anywise appertaining. And all the estate,right, title, and interest, whatsoever, of them the said parties of the first part and their nation, of, in, and to the said tract of land above described, except as is above excepted, to gave and to hold all and singular the said granted premises, with the appurtenances to the said party of the second part, his heirs and assigns, to his and their proper use, benefit and behoof forever.

In witness whereof, the parties to these presents have hereunto interchangeably set their hands and seals, the day and year first above written.

Robert Morris, by his attorney, Thomas Morris,
Koyengquahtah, alias Young King, his x mark,
Soonookshewan, his x mark,
Konutaico, alias Handsome Lake, his x mark,
Sattakanguyase, alias Two Skies of a length, his x mark,
Onayawos, or Farmer's Brother, his x mark,
Soogooyawautau, alias Red Jacket, his x mark,
Gishkaka, alias Little Billy, his x mark,
Kaoundoowana, alias Pollard, his x mark,
Ouneashataikau, or Tall Chief, by his agent, Stevenson, his x mark,
Teahdowainggua, alias Thos. Jemison, his x mark,
Onnonggaiheko, alias Infant, his x mark,
Tekonnondee, his x mark,
Oneghtaugooau, his x mark,
Connawaudeau, his x mark,

Taosstaiefi, his x mark,

Koeentwahka, or Corn Planter, his x mark,

Oosaukaunendauki, alias to Destroy a Town, his x mark,

Sooeoowa, alias Parrot Nose, his x mark,

Toonahookahwa, his x mark,

Howwennounew, his x mark,

Kounahkaetoue, his x mark,

Tauuyaukauna, his x mark,

Woudougoohkta, his x mark,

Sonauhquaukau, his x mark,

Twaunauiyana, his x mark,

Takaunoudea, his x mark,

Shequinedaughque, or Little Beard, his x mark,

Jowaa, his x mark,

Saunajee, his x mark,

Tauoiyuquatakausea, his x mark,

Taoundaudish, his x mark,

Tooauquinda, his x mark,

Ahtaou, his x mark,

Taukooshoondakoo, his x mark,

Kauneskanggo, his x mark,

Soononjuwau, his x mark,

Tonowauiya, or Captain Bullet, his x mark,

Jaahkaaeyas, his x mark,

Taugihshauta, his x mark,

Sukkenjoonau, his x mark,

Ahquatieya, or Hot Bread, his x mark,

Suggonundau, his x mark,

Taunowaintooh, his x mark,

Konnonjoowauna, his x mark,

Soogooeyandestak, his x mark,

Hautwanauekkau, by Young King, his x mark,

Sauwejuwan, his x mark,

Kaunoohshauwen, his x mark,

Taukonondaugekta, his x mark,

Kaouyanoughque, or John Jemison, his x mark,

Hoiegush, his x mark,

Taknaahquau, his x mark,

Sealed and delivered in presence of

Nat. W. Howell,

Joseph Ellicott,

Israel Chapin,

James Rees,

Henry Aaron Hills,

Henry Abeel,

Jaspar Parrish, Horatio Jones,
 Interpreters.

Done at a full and general treaty of the Seneka nation of
Indians, held at Genesee, in the county of Ontario, and
State of New York, on the fifteenth day of September, in
the year of our Lord one thousand seven hundred and
ninety-seven, under the authority of the United States.

In testimony whereof, I have hereunto set my hand and
seal, the day and year aforesaid
Jere. Wadsworth,

Pursuant to a resolution of the legislature of the
Commonwealth of Massachusetts, passed the eleventh
day of March, in the year of our Lord one thousand
seven hundred and ninety-one, I have attended a full
and general treaty of the Seneka nation of Indians, at
Genesee, in the county of Ontario, when the within
instrument was duly executed in my presence by the
sachems, chiefs, and warriors of the said nation, being
fairly and properly understood and transacted by all the
parties of Indians concerned, and declared to be done

to their universal satisfaction: I therefore certify and approve of the same.

William Shepard.
Subscribed in presence of
Nat. W. Howell.

1798 CE Oct. 2

Articles of a treaty between the United Stales of America, and the Cherokee Indians.

WHEREAS, the treaty made and concluded on Holston River, on the second day of July, in the year one thousand seven hundred and ninety-one between the United States of America, and the Cherokee nation of Indians, had not been carried into execution, for some time thereafter, by reason of some misunderstandings which had arisen:—And whereas, in order to remove such misunderstandings, and to provide for carrying the said treaty into effect, and for re-establishing more fully the peace and friendship between the parties, another treaty was held, made and concluded by and between them, at Philadelphia, the twenty-sixth day of June in the year one thousand seven hundred and ninety-four: In which, among other things, it was stipulated, that the boundaries mentioned in the fourth article of the said treaty of Holston, should be actually ascertained and marked, in the manner prescribed by the said article, whenever the Cherokee nation should have ninety days notice of the time and place at which the commissioners of the United States intended to commence their operation: And whereas further delays in carrying the said fourth article into complete effect did take place, so that the boundaries mentioned and described therein, were not regularly ascertained and marked, until the latter part of the year one thousand seven hundred and ninety-seven: before which time, and for want of knowing the direct course of the said boundary, divers settlements were made, by divers citizens of the United States, upon the Indian lands over and beyond the boundaries so mentioned and described in the said article, and contrary to the intention of the said treaties: but which settlers were removed from the said Indian lands by authority of the United States, as soon after the boundaries had been so lawfully ascertained and marked as the nature of the case had admitted:

And whereas, for the purpose of doing justice to the Cherokee nation of Indians and remedying inconveniences arising to citizens of the United States from the adjustment of the boundary line between the lands of the Cherokees and those of the United States, or the citizens thereof, or from any other cause in relation to the Cherokees; and in order to promote the interests and safety of the said states, and the citizens thereof, the President of the United States, by and with the advice and consent of the Senate thereof, hath appointed George Walton, of Georgia, and the President of the United States hath also appointed Lieutenant-Colonel Thomas Butler commanding the troops of the United States in the state of Tennessee, to be commissioners for the purpose aforesaid: And who, on the part of the United States, and the Cherokee nation by the undersigned chiefs and warriors, representing the said nation, have agreed to the following articles, namely:

ARTICLE 1.

The peace and friendship subsisting between the United States and the Cherokee people, are hereby renewed, continued, and declared perpetual.

ARTICLE 2.

The treaties subsisting between the present contracting parties, are acknowledged to be of full and operating force; together with the construction and usage under their respective articles, and so to continue.

ARTICLE 3.

The limits and boundaries of the Cherokee nation, as stipulated and marked by the existing treaties between the parties, shall be and remain the same, where not altered by the present treaty.

ARTICLE 4.

In acknowledgement for the protection of the United
States, and for the considerations hereinafter expressed
and contained, the Cherokee nation agree, and do
hereby relinquish and cede to the United States, all the
lands within the following points and lines, viz. From a
point on the Tennessee river, below Tellico block-house,
called the Wild-cat Rock, in a direct line to the Militia
spring, near the Mary-ville road leading from Tellico.
From the said spring to the Chill-howie mountain, by a
line so to be run, as will leave all the farms on Nine-mile
Creek to the northward and eastward of it; and to be
continued along Chill-howie mountain, until it strikes
Hawkins's line. Thence along the said line to the great
Iron mountain; and from the top of which a line to be
 continued in a southeastwardly course to where the
most southwardly branch of Little river crosses the
divisional line to Tuggaloe river: from the place of
beginning, the Wild-cat Rock, down the northeast
margin of the Tennessee river (not including islands) to
 a point or place one mile above the junction of that
river with the Clinch, and from thence by a line to be

drawn in a right angle, until it intersects Hawkins's line leading from Clinch. Thence down the said line to the river Clinch; thence up the said river to its junction with Emmery's river; and thence up Emmery's river to the foot of Cumberland mountain. From thence a line to be drawn, northeastwardly along the foot of the mountain, until it intersects with Campbell's line.

ARTICLE 5.

To prevent all future misunderstanding about the line described in the foregoing article, two commissioners shall be appointed to superintend the running and marking the same, where not ascertained by the rivers, immediately after signing this treaty; one to be appointed by the commissioners of the United States, and the other by the Cherokee nation; and who shall cause three maps or charts thereof to be made out; one whereof shall be transmitted and deposited in the war office of the United States; another with the executive of the state of Tennessee, and the third with the Cherokee nation, which said line shall form a part of the boundary between the United States and the Cherokee nation.

ARTICLE 6.

In consideration of the relinquishment and cession hereby made, the United States upon signing the present treaty shall cause to be delivered to the Cherokees, goods, wares and merchandise, to the amount of five thousand dollars, and shall cause to be delivered, annually, other goods to the amount of one thousand dollars, in addition to the annuity already provided for; and will continue the guarantee of the remainder of their country forever, as made and contained in former treaties.

ARTICLE 7.

The Cherokee nation agree, that the Kentucky road, running between the Cumberland mountain and the Cumberland river, where the same shall pass through the Indian land, shall be an open and free road for the use of the citizens of the United States in like manner as the road from Southwest point to Cumberland river. In consideration of which it is hereby agreed on the part of the United States, that until settlements shall make it improper, the Cherokee hunters shall be at liberty to hunt and take game upon the lands relinquished and ceded by this treaty.

ARTICLE 8.

Due notice shall be given to the principal towns of the Cherokees, of the time proposed for delivering the annual stipends; and sufficient supplies of provisions shall be furnished, by and at the expense of the United States, to subsist such reasonable number that may be sent, or shall attend to receive them during a reasonable time.

ARTICLE 9.

It is mutually agreed between the parties, that horses stolen and not returned within ninety days, shall be paid for at the rate of sixty dollars each; if stolen by a white man, citizen of the United States, the Indian proprietor shall be paid in cash; and if stolen by an Indian from a citizen, to be deducted as expressed in the fourth article of the treaty of Philadelphia.—This article shall have retrospect to the commencement of the first conferences at this place in the present year, and no further. And all animosities, aggressions, thefts and plunderings, prior to that day shall cease, and be no longer remembered or demanded on either side.

ARTICLE 10.

The Cherokee nation agree, that the agent who shall be appointed to reside among them from time to time, shall have a sufficient piece of ground allotted for his temporary use.

And lastly, This treaty, and the several articles it contains, shall be considered as additional to, and forming a part of, treaties already subsisting between the United States and the Cherokee nation, and shall be carried into effect on both sides, with all good faith as soon as the same shall be approved and ratified by the President of the United States, and the Senate thereof.

In witness of all and every thing herein determined between the United States of America, and the whole Cherokee nation, the parties hereunto set their hands and seals in the council house, near Tellico, on Cherokee ground, and within the United States, this second day of October, in the year one thousand seven hundred and ninety-eight, and in the twenty-third year of the independence and sovereignty of the United States.

Thos. Butler,
Geo. Walton.

Nenetuah, or bloody Fellow, his x mark,
Ostaiah, his x mark,
Jaunne, or John, his x mark,
Oortlokecteh, his x mark,
Chockonnistaller, or Stallion, his x mark,
Noothoietah, his x mark,

Kunnateelah, or Rising Fawn, his x mark,

Utturah, or Skin Worm, his x mark,

Weelee, or Will his x mark,

Oolassoteh, his x mark,

Tlorene, his x mark,

Jonnurteekee, or Little John,

Oonatakoteekee, his x mark,

Kanowsurhee, or Broom, his x mark,

Yonah Oolah, Bear at Home, his x mark,

Tunksalenee, or Thick Legs, his x mark,

Oorkullaukee, his x mark,

Kumamah, or Butterfly, his xmark,

Chattakuteehee, his x mark,

Kanitta, or Little Turkey, his x mark,

Kettegiskie, his x mark,

Tauquotihee, or the Glass, his x mark,

Chuquilatague, his x mark,

Salleekookoolah, his x mark,

Tallotuskee, his x mark,

Chellokee, his x mark,

Tuskeegatee, or Long Fellow, his x mark,

Neekaanneah, or Woman Holder, his x mark,

Kulsateehee, his x mark,

Keetakeuskah, or Prince, his x mark,

Charley, his x mark,

Akooh, his x mark,

Sawanookeh, his x mark,

Yonahequah, or Big Bear, his x mark,

Keenahkunnah, his x mark,

Kaweesoolaskee, his x mark,

Teekakalohenah, his x mark,

Ookouseteeh, or John Taylor, his x mark,

Chochuchee, his x mark,

Witnesses:

Elisha I. Hall, secretary of the commission,

Silas Dinsmoor, Indian agent to the Cherokees,

John W. Hooker, United States factor,

Edw. Butler, captain commanding at Tellico,

Robert Purdy, lieutenant Fourth U. S. Regiment,

Ludwell Grymes,

Jno. McDonald,

Daniel Ross,

Mattw. Wallace, esquire,

Saml. Hanly,

Michael McKinsey,

Chas. Hicks, interpreter,

James Cazey, interpreter,

John Thompson,

1804 CE Mar 26

Congress ordered the removal of Indians east of the Mississippi to Louisiana.

1804 CE Aug 31

Lewis and Clark held a council with local Sioux Indian chiefs in what is now eastern North Dakota.

1804 CE Oct 26

Lewis and Clark accepted an invitation to camp for the winter near a cluster of villages inhabited by the Mandan and Hidatsa Indians.

1804 CE Nov

Lewis and Clark hired French-Canadian fur trapper Toussaint Charbonneau as an interpreter, with the understanding that Sacagawea, who was only about 16 and pregnant, would come along to interpret the Shoshone language. She and another woman had been purchased by Charbonneau, who lived among the Hidatsa and Mandan Indians, to be his wives.

1805 CE July

Chickasaw Treaty

Articles of arrangement made and concluded in the Chickasaw country, between James Robertson and Silas Dinsmoor, commissioners of the United States of the one part, and the Mingo chiefs and warriors of the Chickasaw nation of Indians on the other part.

ARTICLE 1.

WHEREAS the Chickasaw nation of Indians have been for some time embarrassed by heavy debts due to their merchants and traders, and being destitute of funds to effect important improvements in their country, they have agreed and do hereby agree to cede to the United States, and forever quit claim to the tract of country included within the following bounds, to wit: beginning on the left bank of Ohio, at the point where the present Indian boundary adjoins the same, thence down the left bank of Ohio to the Tennessee river, thence up the main channel of the Tennessee river to the mouth of Duck river; thence up the left bank of Duck river to the Columbian highway or road leading from Nashville to Natchez, thence along the said road to the ridge dividing the waters running into Duck river from those running into Buffaloe river, thence easterly along the said ridge to the great ridge dividing the waters running into the main Tennessee river from those running into Buffaloe river near the main source of Buffaloe river, thence in a direct line to the Great Tennessee river near the Chickasaw old fields or eastern point of the Chickasaw claim on that river; thence northwardly to the great ridge dividing the waters running into the Tennessee from those running into Cumberland river, so as to include all the waters running into Elk river, thence along the top of the said great ridge to the place of beginning: reserving a tract of one mile square adjoining to, and below the mouth of Duck river on the Tennessee, for the use of the chief O'Koy or Tishumastubbee.

ARTICLE 2.

The United States on their part, and in consideration of the above cession, agree to make the following payments, to wit: Twenty thousand dollars for the use of the nation at large, and for the payment of the debts due to their merchants and traders; and to George Colbert and O'Koy two thousand dollars, that is, to each one thousand dollars. This sum is granted to them at the request of the national council for services rendered their nation, and is to be subject to their individual order, witnessed by the resident agent; also to Chinubbee Mingo, the king of the nation, an annuity of one hundred dollars, during his natural life, granted as a testimony of his personal worth and friendly disposition. All the above payments are to be made in specie.

ARTICLE 3.

In order to preclude for ever all disputes relative to the boundary mentioned in the first section, it is hereby stipulated, that the same shall be ascertained and marked by a commissioner or commissioners on the part of the United States, accompanied by such person as the Chickasaws may choose, so soon as the Chickasaws shall have thirty days' notice of the time and place, at which the operation is to commence: and the United States will pay the person appointed on the part of the Chickasaws two dollars per day during his actual attendance on that service.

ARTICLE 4.

It is hereby agreed on the part of the United States, that from and after the ratification of these articles, no settlement shall be made by any citizen, or permitted by the government of the United States, on that part of the present cession included between the present Indian boundary and the Tennessee, and between the Ohio and a line drawn due north from the mouth of Buffaloe to the ridge dividing the waters of Cumberland from those of the Tennessee river, to the term of three years.

ARTICLE 5.

The articles now stipulated will be considered as permanent additions to the treaties now in force between the contracting parties, as soon as they shall have been ratified by the President of the United States of America, by and with the advice and consent of the Senate of the said United States.

In witness of all and every thing herein determined, the parties have hereunto interchangeably set their hands and seals, in the Chickasaw country, this twenty-third day of July, in the year of our Lord one thousand eight hundred and five, and of the independence of the United States of America the thirtieth.

Commissioners:

James Robertson

Silas Dinsmoor,

Chiefs and warriors:

Chenubbee Mingo, the king, his x mark,

George Colbert, his x mark,

O Koy, his x mark,

Tiphu Mashtubbee, his x mark,

Choomubbee, his x mark,

Mingo Mattaha, his x mark,

E. Mattaha Meko, his x mark,

Wm. McGillivry, his x mark,

Tisshoo Hooluhta, his x mark, Levi Colbert, his x mark,

Signed, sealed, and interchanged, in presence of

Thomas Augustine Claiborne, secretary to the

commissioners,

W.P. Anderson, of Tennessee.

Malcolm McGee, his x mark,

Samuel Mitchell, United States agent to the Chickasaw

nation

John Pitchlynn,

Christopher Olney,

John McKee,

Wm. Tyrrell,

R. Chamberlin, second lieutenant Second Regiment Infantry, Sworn interpreters.

1805 CE

Prophet's Town

Tecumseh and his younger brother Tenskwatawa (Open Door or the Shawnee Prophet) established a village near present-day Greenville, Ohio in 1805 as a mission for Native American unity.

Upon receiving a vision from the Great Spirit or Master of Life, Tenskwatawa vowed to renounce alcohol and preached to return to traditional Indian practices, native foods, implements, dress, and ceremonies of their ancestors.

Tensions grew as settlers feared the growing contingent living south of the Greene Ville Treaty line.

Pressured by William Henry Harrison, the Prophet moved his followers to the Indiana Prophetstown in 1808, which was destroyed in the ill-fated Battle of Tippecanoe in 1811.

During the Shawnee removal west in 1826, the Prophet asked the U. S. Army for permission to spend a few days here to honor their ancestors.

1805 CE Aug 30

The Lewis and Clark Corps of Discovery resumed their westward journey with 29 horses and 6 guides provided by Shoshoni Chief Cameahwait.

1805 CE Sep 23

Lt. Zebulon Pike purchased 9-sq. miles of land on the mouth of the Minnesota River from the Sioux; paying $2,000; later established Fort Snelling.

1807 CE

Oldtown in Greene County, Ohio — Site of Old Chillicothe Shawnee Village destroyed four times by pioneer forces.

It remained Ohio's leading Indian Town until 1807.

1808 CE, late April

Tecumseh and his brother, The Prophet, move their followers from western Ohio.

To escape white settlers, they travel down the Mississinewa River to north of present day Lafayette of the Tippecanoe River near the mouth of the Wabash River.

Their village, named Prophetstown, poses a major threat to Gov. William Henry Harrison's line of communication between Vincennes and Fort Wayne.

1809 CE September 30

Gov. Harrison negotiates the Treaty of Fort Wayne with the Delaware, Potawatomi, Miami, Wea, Kickapoo and the Eel River tribes, giving the United States title to more than 2 million acres in the southern third of Indiana. Tecumseh is angry at the tribal chiefs' land giveaway.

Treaty of Fort Wayne

Condition
Transfer of money and goods to natives; Natives to allow American settlement of purchased land; Contingent on the later acceptance of the Kickapoo and Wea.

Signatories
William Henry Harrison, Native leaders

Parties
United States of America, Delawares, Potowatomi, Miami, The Eel River band of Miami, Weas (Signed November 1809), Kickapoo (Signed March 1810).

The Treaty of Fort Wayne, sometimes called the Ten O'clock Line Treaty or the Twelve Mile Line Treaty, is an 1809 treaty that obtained 3,000,000 acres of American Indian land for the white settlers of Illinois and Indiana.

The tribes involved were the Delaware, Eel River, Miami tribe, and Potawatomi in the initial negotiations; later Kickapoo and the Wea, who were the primary inhabitants of the region being sold.

The negotiations did not include the Shawnee who were minor inhabitants of the area purchased and had been asked to leave the area previously by Miami War Chief Little Turtle.

Territorial Governor William Henry Harrison negotiated the treaty with the tribes.

The treaty led to a war with the United States began by Shawnee leader Tecumseh and other dissenting tribesmen in what came to be called "Tecumseh's War".

The treaty also has two nicknames, the "Ten O'clock

Line Treaty of 1809" and the "Twelve Mile Line Treaty".

The first nickname comes from tradition that says the Native Americans did not trust the surveyors' equipment, so a spear was thrown down at ten o'clock and the shadow became the treaty line.

There are other myths that say it was either a tree or a fence that was used.

The Twelve Mile Line was a reference to the Greenville Treaty and the establishment of a new 'line' parallel to it but twelve miles further west.

In 1809 Harrison began to push for a treaty to open more land for settlement. The Miami, Wea, and Kickapoo were "vehemently" opposed to selling any more land around the Wabash River.

In order to influence those groups to sell the land, Harrison decided, against the wishes of President James Madison, to first conclude a treaty with the tribes willing to sell and use them to help influence those who held out.

In September 1809 he invited the Pottawatomie, Lenape, Eel Rivers, and the Miami to a meeting in Fort Wayne.

In the negotiations Harrison promised large subsidies and payments to the tribes if they would cede the lands he was asking for.

Only the Miami opposed the treaty.

They presented their copy of the Treaty of Greenville and read the section that guaranteed their possession of the lands around the Wabash River.

They then explained the history of the region and how they had invited the Wea and other tribes to settle in their territory as friends.

The Miami were concerned the Wea leaders were not present, although they were the primary inhabitants of the land being sold.

The Miami also wanted any new land sales to be paid for by the acre, and not by the tract.

Harrison agreed to make the treaty's acceptance contingent on approval by the Wea and other tribes in the territory being purchased, but he refused to purchase land by the acre.

He countered that it was better for the tribes to sell the land in tracts so as to prevent the Americans from only purchasing their best lands by the acre and leaving them only poor land to live on.

After two weeks of negotiating, the Pottawatomie leaders convinced the Miami to accept the treaty as reciprocity to the Pottawatomie who had earlier accepted treaties less advantageous to them at the request of the Miami.

Finally the Treaty of Fort Wayne was signed on September 29, 1809, selling United States over 3,000,000 acres, chiefly along the Wabash River north of Vincennes.

During the winter months, Harrison was able to obtain the acceptance of the Wea by offering them a large subsidy and the help of Miami Chief Pacanne who helped to influence the Wea leaders.

The Kickapoo were closely allied with the Shawnee at Prophetstown and Harrison feared they would be difficult to sway.

He offered the Wea an increased subsidy if the Kickapoo would also accept the treaty, causing the Wea to pressure the Kickapoo leaders to accept.

By the spring of 1810 Harrison had completed negotiations and the treaty was finalized.

1811 CE

Gen. William Henry Harrison won a battle against the Shawnee Indians at the Battle of Tippecanoe in the Indiana territory.

1811 CE November 7

Prophetstown Indians attack Gen. William Henry Harrison's force of 760, killing 60 and injuring 128 people.

Harrison estimates more than 100 Indians are killed. The Kickapoos say 25 of their tribe are killed.

Harrison destroys the stronghold and cornfields at Prophetstown, angering and scattering Tecumseh's followers.

1812 CE

Hull's Headquarters was in Urbana, Champaign County.

Gen. William Hull largely recruited his army for his campaign against the British at Detroit, in the War of 1812.

General Hull surrendered Detroit, without a shot, to a small British force under Sir Isaac Brock.

For his actions, General Hull was court martialled and sentenced to death by firing squad, but President James Madison pardoned him.

1812 CE

Much of the area of present-day Allen County was originally Ottawa territory.

The soil was rich and there were natural springs and salt licks.

To prevent a possible invasion of Ohio, Gen. William Henry
Harrison, commander of the Northwestern Army, called up the Kentucky and Ohio militia.

Rather than moving troops and supplies across the Black Swamp, he chose to use the Auglaize and St. Marys rivers.

Native Americans refused to live in the foreboding region of the Black Swamp.

They would go into the swamp lands to hunt, but this was at great peril.

If they didn't stay on a previously blazed trail, they risked the danger of becoming hopelessly lost in the dense under and over growth, and for much of the year, the land was flooded.

Water, often up to the belly of a horse, stood on the surface until it evaporated. When it rained, or thawed in the winter, it was water and muck.

Much of the swamp was covered with an almost impenetrable forest of giant oak, sycamore, hickory, walnut, ash, elm, maple and cottonwood trees, except in a few prairie areas where limestone just under the surface would not support timber growth.

It is hard to believe that there once lay a terrible swamp 40 miles wide and 120 miles long - an oozing mass of water, mud, snakes, wolves, wildcats, biting flies, and clouds of gnats and mosquitoes - big enough to cover the entire area of the states of Rhode Island and Delaware and nearly 40% of Connecticut, combined!

In November 1812 Harrison ordered Lt. Robert Pogue of the Kentucky Mounted Militia to construct a supply depot at this site, previously an Ottawa village.

Quickly built, Fort Amanda initially consisted of four two story blockhouses connected by 11-foot palisades, occupying an area of about 160 feet by 160 feet.

Capt. Thomas Ward's company of Kentucky militia garrisoned the fort until February 1813, when Capt. Daniel Hosbrook of the Ohio militia assumed command.

Under his direction the fort was enlarged to accommodate the growing quantity of supplies stored here, which included livestock, grain, munitions, and whiskey.

The camp became a key debarkation point for soldiers and supplies heading north in the effort to recapture Detroit.

Fort Amanda was abandoned by early 1815 and was subsequently occupied by local settlers.

1812 CE, May 15

Twelve Indian nations hold grand council with Tecumseh at Mississinewa village at the junction of the Wabash and Mississinewa rivers near present-day Peru, Indiana.

The Wyandots, Miami, Potawatomies, Delaware and Kickapoos urge Tecumseh to restrain his young warriors lest all tribes suffer at the hands of the whites.

Tecumseh denies that his followers are a threat to the whites and rebukes the chiefs for selling their people out at the Treaty of Fort Wayne.

1812 CE June 19

The United States declares war on Great Britain.

1812 CE, July 14

Miami war chief Little Turtle dies and with his death United States' influence upon the Miami Indians and other tribes in Indian territory evaporates.

1812 CE, July 17

The British capture the fort on Mackinac Island with the aid of the Indian tribes. For all practical purposes, the United States loses control of lakes Michigan and Huron.

1812 CE, August 15

Potawatomi force the surrender of Fort Dearborn (Chicago) and massacre most of the garrison being evacuated by William Wells, adopted son of Little Turtle.

1812 CE, August 16

In a devastating blow to the United States, Gen. William Hull surrenders Fort Detroit and the Army of the Northwest to forces led by British General William Brock and Tecumseh.

Most tribal chiefs lose control over their young warriors as Tecumseh emerges as the new Indiana leader in the Northwest Territory.

Armed whites and Indians attack each other throughout Illinois, Indiana and Ohio.

Killing becomes commonplace among the two peoples.

1812 CE, August 18

Unable to control their warriors, tribal chiefs refuse Harrison's invitation to attend a peace council at Piqua, Ohio.

1812 CE, September 3

The Shawnees led by Missilimeta ravage the Pigeon Roost settlement in southern Indiana, killing 20 whites.

1812 CE, September 6

Indians attack Fort Wayne and Fort Harrison (Terre Haute). The Americans successfully withstand the attacks.

In turn, the Americans raid and destroy Indian villages north of the Wabash River.

1812 CE, September 24

Harrison is given command of the second Army of the Northwest, replacing Gen. James Winchester.

1812 CE, October 11

Indiana Agent B. F. Stickney passes along information from trader John Conner to Harrison.

From Sept. 13 to Oct. 2, the Miamis have sent nine messengers to the Delawares, inviting them to join them in war against the United States.

1812 CE, October 26

Harrison seeks approval from Secretary of War William Eustis to attack the Indian towns on the Mississinewa River.

1812 CE, November 5

Secretary Eustis advises Harrison that "the Miamis, as well as the other Indians, must be dealt with as their merits and demerits may in your judgment require."

1812 CE, November 15

Informed of Gen. Samuel Hopkins' defeat in Illinois and the growing confidence of the Indians in attacking the Army's supply lines, Harrison advises Eustis that he will command Col. John B. Campbell to direct an expedition against the Miami town of Mississinewa.

It will be the rendezvous where the Indians are certain to receive provisions and assistance in launching attacks on every military convoy in Ohio between St. Mary's and the Miami Rapids (present-day Maumee).

1812 CE, November 22

Gen. Hopkin's force destroys Prophetstown along with deserted Winnebago and Kickapoo villages along the Tippecanoe River.

The Indians ambush and kill 16 of Hopkins' force on Wildcat Creek, north-west of present-day Kokomo.

1812 CE, November 25

Harrison orders Campbell to attack and destroy the Miami village at Mississinewa.

Campbell is advised to try to spare chiefs Richardville, Silver Heels, White Loon, Charley and Pecon, and the sons and daughters of Little Turtle if it can be done without risk to his force.

He is also advised to guarantee the safety of the Indian women and children who are to be captured and conducted back to settlements in Ohio--a condition that will eventually cost Campbell severe losses among his troops.

1812 CE, December 14

Campbell's force of nearly 600 mounted troops, guided by William Conner, departs Fort Greenville, Ohio, on an 80-mile forced march to the Miami towns on the Mississinewa River. The snow is knee deep, and the weather is bitter cold.

1812 CE, December 17

Campbell's force surprises and attacks the first of four Indian villages on the Mississinewa River near present-day Jalapa.

Eight Indians and one African-American are killed. Forty-two Indians, including 34 women and children, are captured.

Two American solders lose their lives.

1812 CE, December 18

Just before dawn, a force of about 300 Indians counterattack, killing eight soldiers and wounding 48.

Fifteen Indians are killed.

Faced with bitter cold weather, mounting casualties due to frostbite and the loss of 109 horses killed in battle, Campbell withdraws his forces to Greenville.

1812 CE, December 24

His troops decimated by freezing weather, Campbell's force arrives at Greenville.

More than 300 of his troops are victims of frostbite when Campbell allows the Indian women and children to ride captured Indian horses on the return trip.

The captives are escorted to Indian settlements at Piqua.

1813 CE, Aug. 18

Henry and Barbara Dilbone who were killed by the Indians on their farm; Miami County, Ohio.

All of Nature has the wisdom to follow the Natural Laws.

All of Nature knows how to live in harmony and use this wisdom in a good way, with exception of the human being.

Often we misuse this wisdom.

Wisdom always remains with those who use it in the proper way.

Nature has used this wisdom well, so now we need to go to Her so we humans can relearn and change our lives.

May we start doing this today, before it is too late.

Mist of A Different Fire

Up to this point, we have reviewed the association of the "white man" with the "Indian" across the span of time – beginning with DNA research finding "95% of all native Americans descend from 6 Asian women" whose descendents crossed a land bridge from Asia into North America some eighteen to twenty-one thousand years before the common era; putting Amerindians on the North American continent tens of thousands of years before the 'white man' exploration.

The book then concludes with the August 18, 1813 "Dilbone Massacre" near present-day Piqua, Ohio, Miami County.

What can be seen is this:

Native Americans have a history here in the United States far greater than the white man – 23,000 years.

Additionally, neither "side" is above savage acts; nor is neither side "savage" at all times. Both had a 'superior' mind-set over the other.

But, what does all this tie-in with the subject of "The Dilbone Massacre of 1813"?

Let's begin with the *concept of "Manifest Destiny"*.

With the "superiority" of the 'white man' being previously stated herein, don't you think Native Americans were also capable of the same mindset?

Absolutely, they were!....

- *The virtue of the Native American people and their institutions;*

- *The mission to spread these institutions, thereby redeeming and remaking the world in the image of the Indian Nation;*

- *The destiny under the Grandfather to do this work.*

What can be stated, then, is this:

Most societies have stories and traditions which are handed down from generation to generation; whether by written word or word-of-mouth.

These 'family' stories can provide many clues to further research, but you need to approach them with an open mind.

Just because your Great-Grandma says that it happened that way, doesn't make it so!

Just because it is a written document, doesn't necessarily make it so, either.

In other words, to get to the truth of long-ago days, one must separate fact from fiction.

For example:

I have actively studied my family genealogy for almost fifteen years.

Oral family history on my paternal side was that my great-grandparents "died in a farmhouse fire somewhere around Troy, Ohio".

Having since found documented evidence, I discovered this to be only *partially* true:

They lived in Troy-proper in 1891.

My paternal great-father died.

He was poisoned by carbon monoxide in the early days of home heat gases.

The flu pipe damper was found to be fully closed.

The question, however, remains: Did he know or not know what he was doing that fateful night?

Stories like ghost stories, stories about famous ancestors, war heroes, surname changes, or the family's nationality, all probably have their roots in fact.

The "job" of the seeker of truth is to sort out these facts from the fiction - having likely grown as embellishments added over time - to stories.

A handful of accounts of the Dilbone Massacre have been written; and while they differ in their story structure, facts and embellishments, the conclusion remains the same: Henry and Barbara Dilbone were killed.

It is because of these differences, and as one who studies history and genealogy, I question the facts and attempt to sort them from embellishments.

With this in mind, I have compared the differences and similarities in the various historical accounts of the "Dilbone Massacre" and come to this conclusion:

Most of the documented history can be combined, oftentimes verbatim, depicting the same outcome for the Dilbone's.

And yet, amongst the documented evidence I've seen two, perhaps three differing evidences of "who done it" and what happened to the "accused".

"[The Dilbone's]....suffered at the hands of the same two Indians who caused his [Garrard] death." (meaning Mingo George and a lad).

Another story tells us, the killing was done by Chief Pashetowa and two or three braves in concert with coordinated raids at the same time.

Garrard, it is written, was killed around noon; The Dilbone's, around 4PM. History documents also state John Dilbone, seven year-old son of the Dilbbone's, heard a shot in the distance, scaring away the Indians.

The suspect, Mingo George, was killed in one story by a search party and stuffed in the mud of the Miami River.

Another story has him being accidently shot by an Indian during a deer hunt.

In another accounting of the story, a Shawnee Chief may or may not have been the killer.

And still, another story states the killer of the Dilbone's was never found!

....the raiders were not identified but were believed to be amongst the Shawnees who were trying to build support for Tecumseh and the Confederation that he was building amongst the Western tribes.

The defeat of the Native tribes by General Wayne had given the Americans control over the southern watershed and the Great Miami River which helped to influence trade for the settlers who were moving into the area.

Tecumseh believed that he could push the settlers out of the Shawnee tribal lands and back across the Appalachians.

Pashetowa, Mingo George and several others attacked the settlers as they worked their flax fields.

Mingo George was known in the area but it has never been clear if he was a resident of the area.

There has never been anything stated of who actually killed Mrs. Dilbone, but accounts do indicate that she did identify Mingo George.

The whole thrust of the attacks was to upset the tentative balance that Colonel John Johnston had been able to create the non-support of Tecumseh's Confederation within the Shawnee tribes living in the area between Piqua and Fort Wayne, IN.

During this time Johnston had called the Council of Piqua together, inviting leaders from the Shawnee tribes and the point of the Council was to seek a pledge of neutrality from the Native Americans.

Mingo George and Chief Pashetowa apparently thought that their actions would cause a reaction by the settlers and the Shawnee would bear the brunt of the retaliation and join Tecumseh and the British and fight against the Americans. - S. Greggerson (personal e-mail) June 15, 2014.

The truly unanswered questions to reflect upon are:

Was "Mingo George" (known by first name and sight to locals) really the killer?

Seven-year-old, John Dilbone, "points the finger" at Mingo George a local native Indian.

Barbara Dilbone screams, "Don't shoot George!"

We know from history, the Indians living in the Miami Valley by this time (1813), were mostly "friendly" to the settlers; likewise, the settlers were friendly with the Indians.

We also know, some 6,000 natives were "housed" at the Johnston Indian Agency.

And while both sides often did trading with the other, We also know there was dissension and anamosity on "both sides":

Some Tribal Chief's did not trust the "whites"; some "whites" did not trust the "savages".

Henry Dilbone, while "being cordial" with the local natives, made "no bones" about his disdain for Tecumseh and other Indians. Tecumseh made "no bones" about his distrust of the "whites".

Thus, the only conclusive evidence readily seen from the context of this book is this:

Which historical documents should one believe... the ones having Mingo George as the killer... or Chief Pashetowa and his braves, whereby Mingo George may or may not have taken part in the massacre?

Was Mingo George killed by a "posse" of settlers, or on a deer hunt, or not killed at all (some documents state the killers were never found)?

"The basis of knowledge is the fire, rock, water, and green. But when that power was given to man, he used it to twist his own mind. Tunkashila (God) gave man just one drop of that wisdom."

--Wallace Black Elk, LAKOTA

Epilogue

The momentum began in Europe and swept the world, burying in its path the aborigines on other continents, including the Americas, whose progress throughout time had remained slow.

Although, in some cases they advanced as providers for their families, their way of life remained virtually unchanged from that of their ancestors.

Their spirits, economics, religion, and way of life was tied inextricably to the land.

Such a place was North America where life began each day with the natives believing that the land was in their guardianship.

Its inhabitants, while not always friendly toward each other, lived pastoral lives of relative simplicity.

Although tribal warfare erupted occasionally among the Indian tribes, their greatest threat came from inclement weather and the shortage of food and water.

'Progress' had passed them by.

Many of today's modern cities are near old Indian villages, a reminder of just how fleeting civilization can be.

Indian towns were communities in every sense of the word, where people married, raised their children, worried, rejoiced, fought and died — just like the 'white people'.

Today, children still play act as cowboys and Indians, pitting the 'good' guys against the 'bad', when in reality, the relationship between the first settlers and the Indian inhabitants was very complex – A relationship where the aggressor and the victim has not always been easy to identify – A relationship of "Manifest Destiny" mind-set on all fronts - *The mist of a different fire - burns with truth.*

REFERENCES CITED

"American Indian Wars" NativeAmericanEncyclopedia.com Unabridged. Native American Encyclopedia 28 May. 2014.

http://digital.library.okstate.edu/kappler/

http://en.wikipedia.org/wiki/Manifest_Destiny

The Historical Marker Database: http://www.hmdb.org/

The History of Miami County, Ohio; W.H. Beers

Indian Affairs : Laws and Treaties Vol II (Treaties) Compiled and Edited By Charles J. Kappler LL. M. Clerk to the Senate Committee on Indian Affairs Washington, DC : Government Printing Office, 1904

Memoirs of The Miami Valley; Robert O. Law Co.

Native American Indian Center of Central Ohio, INC. June 14, 2014

http://nativeamericanencyclopedia.com/american-indian-wars/

NativeAmericanEncyclopedia.com - Elder's Meditation of the Day May 31, 2014

www.nativeamericanencyclopedia.com/history-timeline-the-ohio-indians/

www//mentalfloss.com/article/12657/was-manhattan-really-bought-24

http://www.mississinewa1812.com/timeline.htm

http://www.shelbycountyhistory.org/schs/indians/1783-90revwrovr.htm

http://www.waymarking.com/

www.ingramcontent.com/pod-product-compliance
Lightning Source LLC
Chambersburg PA
CBHW050435290526
45786CB00006B/2045